If You Could Be Anything, What Would You Be?

N

If You Could Be Anything, What Would You Be?

A TEEN'S GUIDE TO MAPPING OUT THE FUTURE

Jeanne Webster, C.P.C.

"To provide teens with the necessary skills,
tools, and strategies to fulfill their potential
so they may lead abundant and exceptional lives."

DUPUIS NORTH PUBLISHING COMPANY
www.youcouldbeanything.com

If You Could Be Anything, What Would You Be?
A TEEN'S GUIDE TO MAPPING OUT THE FUTURE

First Edition
10 9 8 7 6 5 4 3 2 1

Printed in the United States of America

Library of Congress Number: 2004090423

The Life Map was revised and modeled from the
Design Your Life Program©, copyright 2002
International Coach Academy Pty. Ltd.
Use is governed by the terms and conditions at
www.icoachacademy.com.
Last updated July 2002 by Robyn Logan.

CONTENTS

ACKNOWLEDGEMENTS

Any action you take in this world begins with a single idea that moves forward into word and then farther still into reality. That reality begins to ripple out and include and affect other people. This book started out as a small thought that passed through my head. From then until now, it has expanded to include many other people. A book may be written by just one person, but publishing is done by a team.

I have had the privilege to work with a team of individuals who in my opinion are the finest in the business. Without any one of them, this project would not be what it is today. I feel extremely blessed. This small token of acknowledgement does not seem adequate to express my gratitude.

Nothing would be complete without first giving thanks to Creator, coauthor of my life. You know me completely and have given me voice. My continued prayer is for these pages to affect others in the original spirit of my intent for them: to contribute and serve for the highest good of all.

To Claude, my best friend, partner, and husband, where do I begin? Your belief in my abilities humbles me. You have cooked, cleaned, done laundry, served me lunches, and generally kept house and home together while I wrote. Your support and encouragement have been unfailing. Your praise and loving guidance sustain me still. No rose could be as beautiful or chocolate as sweet as the gift of everyday romance you bring to our lives. This book was possible because you made it possible. I am a better person with you than I would ever be without you.

To my children, my treasures, Nick and Sara: What times we have had together! I feel more than privileged to have you as my children. I am honored to have witnessed and shared in your growth and in your lives. Thank you for all the lessons and experiences. Thank you for all the laughter, tears, good times, and hard times. You shaped me as much as I shaped you. We have always upheld each other, and your support in this book has been constant. The adventures of our lives are not over yet.

To Larry Stuenkel: It is divine guidance that you were the first person we talked to about publishing a book. You agreed to talk to perfect strangers over a lunch and generously gave us your time and wisdom. Every person you recommended to us, without exception, has been the cream of the crop. Because of you, the journey of this book has been straight and true. Thank you so much for your giving nature. Not many would have done so much and asked nothing in return.

To Bob Erdmann: Every project has a person who is key to its success. You are the key to this one. We hit the jackpot when we associated with you. Not only did you construct a brilliant marketing plan, but your consultation and continued guidance is the breath that gave this book life. To me you are the definitive expert in publishing and my guru. You're always there for my questions. Your sense of humor makes working with you a pleasure, even though your taste in football teams leaves a lot to be desired! Thank you hardly seems adequate. I enjoy and value the friendship we have forged through this project.

To Mark Sankey: You're not even my publisher and you didn't have to take my call, but you did. You are another example of the spirit of generosity we have been met with while pursuing this dream. You have never been too busy to speak with me. You not only answer my questions but go beyond to educate me in this industry. Whether we are truly related or not, speaking to you feels like family. Thanks, cousin.

To Dianne Nelson: Working with you has been like working with your best girlfriend. Witnessing your creative genius has been a privilege. Another truly essential foundation person on our team: where would I be without you? A meticulous editor and gifted designer, you have made my scribbling into a more beautiful book than I would have believed possible. I call you at the oddest moments and you're there with advice and support. I write you disjointed, rambling e-mails and you somehow make sense of them. You have shared my excitement and calmed my fears. Most of all, you make this fun. Let's do this again!

To Clint Greenleaf: After all the writing, editing, designing, marketing, and publicity are laid in place, you need to get your book printed and in the hands of the consumer. This is almost impossible without a great distributor. For me this is Greenleaf Book Group. Thank goodness you agreed to represent my book. Clint, you make this all seem so easy, and you do it with style and great humor. You make me feel like I am the only client you have. There is such a willingness to nurture and coach your authors with advice, ideas, knowledge, and the benefit of your own expertise. I look forward to a long association with you. Thanks so much!

To Carol Satterlee: My coach, coaching partner, and dear friend. It may have been fate for us to meet in school. It was my lucky day to have you as my coach. It is an honor to have you as a friend. You have supported this project from the moment it was only a dream. You challenged me to make it a goal, and you have continuously enthused me in the process. You are one of the few people in my life I feel is totally on my side and works to help me become everything I want to become. Thank you for being my friend and partner. Thanks, too, to you daughter Allison, whose honest feedback and review of the manuscript was invaluable. How she managed with so many misspelled words I will never know. Here's to a lifetime of collaboration and friendship.

To Robbie Zell: Thank you for all the great photographs and the back cover portrait you did for the book. Thanks, too, for taking the time to get the formatting perfect.

To the many friends at the Mountain Man Restaurant, Rabun County Community Players, and other individuals: Greg Ziegler for your input and advice; Nick Wylie for the computer lessons; Holly Wylie for the grammar checks; J&M Printing for printing anything I wanted at the moment I asked; the ladies at Books Unlimited; and anyone else who gave me encouragement and advice. Thanks for sharing daily our struggles and triumphs while producing this book. Your encouragement and excitement for us means a lot. For all of you who promised to buy the first copy of the book—here's your chance!

Once again, thank you all!

This book is dedicated to my mom,

E. June Phelps.

No one could have asked for a better mother

or a better friend.

"The mother lives in the daughter."

Before You Begin

Within this book you are going to find lots of questions. More than you would usually find in a book. If you have had the opportunity to work with a life coach, you will understand why. For those of you who haven't had the opportunity to work with a life coach, coaches come to their profession believing that you, as an individual, possess all the answers to your questions, doubts, and problems. Coaching is a process that helps you clear your own path.

We begin by agreeing that you are the expert on your life. Whatever roadblocks or problems you are dealing with in your life, we don't have the answers. What we do have are the questions that will enable you to bring forth your own answers and solutions to those roadblocks or problems. By asking questions, we help you widen and reframe your perspectives, clarify your goals, enthuse your dreams, and encourage you to be more than what you are today.

The role I play in this book is mentor/coach. Believe it or not, I was young once and went through what you are going through now. I got to relive the experience parenting my own children through these years. Because my specialty is teen/parent coaching, I feel strongly that I need to reach back with my experience and my profession and point out the joys and the pitfalls that accompany this time in your life. If it makes your life easier and enables you to travel faster and further than me, then my personal goal has been accomplished.

So get ready to entertain a lot of questions. I am interested in what you believe and feel. This book is all about you. Have fun with it!

"Think of work as a vocation
It comes from the Latin word for calling
Which comes from the word voice.
In those meanings it touches on what work really should be.
It should be something that calls to you, as something
you want to do, and it should be something that gives voice
to who you are and what you want to say to the world.
A vocation fills you with a sense of meaning.
It is something that you choose because of what
it allows you to say with your life.
It is, above all else, something that lets you love.

—Excerpted from Letters To My Son *by Kent Nerburnb.*
Reprinted with permission of New World Library.
www.newworldlibrary.com

N

Λ

CHAPTER ONE

The Trip of A Lifetime

HOW BIG IS YOUR DREAM?

> *"Most people die with their music still inside them."*
> — *Benjamin Disraeli*

What if I told you that everything you have ever wanted in life could be yours? That big house with the swimming pool out back, the ski lodge in Aspen, the designer clothes—all of this and more could be part of your life. What would it feel like to know that everything you dream about today could be part of your tomorrow? Well, it can be; and those dreams can become your reality, not by luck or chance or someone waving a magic wand, but by directing your own potential. Do you see yourself as a top fashion designer with fame and recognition or the head of a worldwide banking system? What would it feel like to drive a slick silver Porsche down Rodeo Drive? Perhaps money isn't your driving motivator. How would you feel if you could find the cure for a deadly disease or produce a new power source that will lead us into a more ecologically sound future? Let your mind wander a minute and recall the pictures you have stored in your head of your most perfect life. You can have it!

If you accepted your dreams of a perfect life as unobtainable, then stop this minute and accept them as pure possibility. Everything that has ever been done, invented, created, written, or achieved has started out in someone's dreams. Those dreams were once just an idea, thought, or desire. The difference between your dreams staying just dreams or becoming a reality is believing in yourself and owning the tools to make those dreams become real.

I am going to show you the tools you need to achieve your dreams. You are able to turn those dreams into goals and attain them, no matter how overwhelming and insurmountable they may seem.

BELIEVE IN YOUR GREATNESS

I believe that each of you is destined for greatness. You are born with the seeds of it. I also believe that you form your own fate through the choices you make every day. The fact that you picked this book up is no accident; you were meant to read it and become aware of the principles and tools that lie within it.

This book may be the first step in guiding you to discover and share your individual greatness with a waiting world. I will show you how to take control of your fate and direct it so that your greatness can evolve. I will invite you to invest yourself and your future perfect life by beginning to direct your greatness right at this very moment. How can you go do this? *By taking one step at a time.*

TAKE ONE STEP AT A TIME

Your dream, and living your greatness, may look overwhelming and unachievable at first glance. However, if you break it down into small steps, it will allow you to tackle the task, one portion at a time, and accomplish it.

Once you graduate from school, whether it is high school or college, you are going to be handed a great challenge. It will be to accomplish your dreams and goals over the course of your lifetime. This task is going to look so big, you are going to want to tackle it as fast as you can. You may even try to do everything all at once. Not a good idea.

The better idea is to look at the whole situation and study it a bit. Choose your starting point. Plan out the methods you will use to work toward your goals. You may find that, after you have started, you don't like the point from which you began, or you may not be able to go further in your plan of attack. You may have to stop, rearrange your choices, and start again from a different angle.

It may even strike you at times that you're proceeding way too slowly. But slowly is a whole lot better than tackling the whole thing all at once and realizing you can't deal with it.

TAKE THE TIME YOU NEED FOR LEARNING

Right now you may be so busy learning and growing that you have never given a thought to the direction your life is heading. You may have dreams about what you want your life to look like and what your perfect life would include. But there may be a large gap between *dreaming* about it and how you will actually *achieve* it. Learning *now* how to direct your actions toward obtaining a future perfect life will be a *vital* part of that accomplishment.

Up until the point of your graduation, you will be busy learning. Your parents, church, and teachers all formed a coalition whose goal was to educate you so that you would be armed with the knowledge to achieve your ambitions. You have or will have learned math, sciences, history, English, geography, music, literature, and maybe even a different language other than your own. Your brains are teeming with facts and figures, nouns and adjectives, dates and data. Learn, learn, learn may seem like all you have been doing since the day you were born. If you feel that way, you're right.

There is a tremendous amount you need to know before you can even begin to think about your objectives. Like walking and talking, for starters.

Those two skills come in rather handy. The point is, you had to learn to do those things and you had help and guidance when you were ready to learn them. That is what parents and grandparents, teachers and ministers, coaches and counselors are for.

DEVELOP YOUR OWN STANDARDS

While you were learning the fundamentals, you also had rules set down for you. When you were little they may have been referred to as the "no-no's." At first they were simple. Remember when you got near the stove while your mom was cooking? That was a "no-no." The reason behind the rule was fairly clear. You may have easily touched the stove or pulled a cooking pot down on yourself and been badly burned. Those are protection rules.

As you grow and mature, the list of rules also matures; it becomes more refined and subtle. The "no-no's" turn into the "there will nots." There will be no running in the hallways. There will be no gum chewing, pulling of hair, kicking, biting, or talking out loud in class. The reasons behind those rules are also fairly easy to figure out. They too, were for your protection as well as for everyone else's. When you become independent and take over your own life, the list will change again. This time it will be called the "I will not" list.

> *"If you limit your choices only to what seems possible or reasonable, you disconnect yourself from what you truly want, and all that is left is compromise.*
> *—Robert Fritz*

When you are out on your own, you will have the opportunity to develop and adhere to a set of standards for which you will be responsible. The point I am trying to make is that for the vast majority of your life so far, you have spent your time learning. While you were busy doing that, the adults around you guided you and protected you with rules for you to follow.

N

THINK FOR YOURSELF

Now I am going to invite you to do something besides learning. I am going to invite you to think— not the studying kind of thinking or the memorizing kind of thinking, but the "think for yourself" kind of thinking, and my all-time favorite, the "dreaming" kind of thinking.

I am going to ask you some questions that I want you to really think about. I am also going to ask you to think deeply and fully about your answers to those questions. Most importantly, I want you to think for *yourself*. Your answers cannot be what you think I would like to hear, or what your parents might answer, or what your best friend thinks is cool. I want to know what you truly believe and think and dream about.

I am asking you to read this book and do the exercises because I believe you need an education and an awareness of *conscious thought* to live your life fully. I believe you need guidance and rules to live your life in society in a good way. I also believe you need to dream really wonderful, lovely, large dreams to live your life in a most extraordinary way. You need to become totally aware and conscious of just exactly what *you* want included in the dream of *your* perfect life.

In order to do this, you need to know yourself. In order to do that, you need to think. I believe that, you are being taught to learn, you are not being taught to think. Therefore, it became one of my dreams to devise a method by which I could stimulate you to begin to think about your life and how you want to live it. I want to do this before you find yourself out in the real world, facing situations that you had no part in planning.

KNOW WHO YOU ARE

I dream of you entering the independent phase of your life, fully prepared and fully focused. To do that, you need to know who you are and what you stand for. I want you to have a clear idea of what your perfect life would be and give you the tools to design a perfect life for yourself. I want you to be able to make goals and achieve them. I want you to know that sometimes the road to that achievement is hard and full of roadblocks. I will show you how to move around or just plain run over those roadblocks, so they won't stop you.

I would like you to look at failure, not as an end point, but as a new beginning, and see mistakes as just another form of learning. My dream is for you to live your life with passion and excitement. I would like you to get up every morning, full of energy, happy with who you have become and loving the life you choose to live.

WHAT THIS BOOK IS ALL ABOUT

Having said all that, let me make something clear for you. This book is not intended to push you. I am not presuming to tell you to have a clear idea about your future at any specific age. I don't know how old you are. You may be in ninth grade and just starting your high school years. You may be a senior, ready to graduate. I don't know if you purchased this book yourself or if your parents or mentor purchased it for you. However, I do know why I wrote this book.

I wrote it to be a tool and resource to support you. It is meant to be a *guide*, not a project. If you begin reading and feel as if you don't want to do the exercises, or you're not ready to do them, then please don't. Skip them until you feel that you are ready to tackle the idea of planning your future. If you feel that you know the answers to just a few of the questions, then answer those and leave the others blank. Go back and fill in the rest as they come to you.

This book is about discovery, not about knowing. You may feel one way about something today, and a year from now you may feel totally different about the same subject. Go ahead and change your answers. I encourage you to change and grow.

Every person has his or her internal clock. Because you are the expert on your life, only you can know when you are ready to look into your future. In fact, if you do go to college, your major will probably change at least three times before you graduate.

This book is not intended to get you on a fixed path at this point in your life. Its purpose is to reassure you of your limitless potential. This is about your choices and dreams, with a bit of help toward achieving them. I would like you to think about who you are and discover that you're really wonderful and full of talent.

Be aware that your future is your choice and must always be your choice. Understand that as you are *making* choices today, you should be *aware* that you are making choices. Base your choices on whether or not your actions will continue to support your tomorrow. The consequence of making a choice based on a whim, and not on awareness, is that the choice you make may block a potential future path you may want to pursue.

In this book I am *your* coach. I am not your parent's coach, your teacher's coach, or even your best friend's coach. As *your* coach, I am concerned about *your* wants, needs, and goals. If someone else bought this book for you, then have them read this chapter.

I want you to keep this book a long time. Refer to it as a friend or guide to help you along your path. Make it a diary of your dreams and ideas, not a forced blueprint of how you must plan and live your life tomorrow. Play with it and have fun with it. Take your time designing your life. Allow yourself to incorporate changes as you move through these formative years. Don't let life just happen to you. Believe that you have the ability to create a life that will bring you joy and value.

"Yes I am a dreamer. For a dreamer is one who can find his way by moonlight, and see the dawn before the rest of the world.
—Oscar Wilde

I am living my dream and sharing my passion for my work with you at this very moment. I want the same for you. So I invite you to get excited about this book. I invite you to think your highest thoughts about who you are and who you can become. Most of all, I invite you to invest in your dream.

N

CHAPTER TWO

Choosing A Destination

SO WHAT IS YOUR DREAM?

> *"We are called to be the architects of the future,*
> *not its victims.*
> *—Buckminster Fuller*

S o what is your dream? I am sure all of you have at one time or another
dreamed about what you want to do when you get out of school. Do
you want to be a doctor or maybe a teacher? Are you good at fixing things, or
are you interested in how they work? If so, perhaps you would like to be a
mechanic or an engineer. If you could live anywhere, where would you choose
to live? Do you see yourself married with children?

BE CLEAR ABOUT YOUR DREAM

All of these decisions will come up for you as you move out into the world
and begin to live for yourself. Wouldn't it be great to go out there prepared with
some clear idea of the answers to those questions? Not just off-the-top-of-your-

head answers, but well-thought-out and well-planned answers. I want you to be clear on what you're dreaming about. Let me share the experience I had with off-the-top-of-my-head answers.

When I was young, someone asked what I wanted to do when I got out of school. It was the first time anyone had asked me that question, and I felt I would look stupid or undirected if I answered that I didn't know yet. I really had not thought about what direction I wanted my life to take, nor had I thought about possible careers. I quickly ran over the list of professions I was aware of and answered that I wanted to be a teacher. It sounded like a reasonable answer to me and, having said it, I just stuck with the teacher choice whenever the question came up. Little did I know it would have been wiser to simply answer the question with the truth. *I didn't know yet.* Once I claimed teaching as my profession, it stuck. I even started college with teaching as my major.

When I began to realize some things about myself, I understood that teaching in a school environment wasn't for me. I don't like working for someone else. I don't like having a set schedule or getting up early in the morning. Soon the list of "don't likes" about teaching was a lot longer than the list of things I did like. I soon realized I would have been miserable as a teacher and, in turn, I would have been a lousy teacher.

I was into my second year in college before I had this revelation and decided to switch my major. I felt badly that I had already taken classes toward a teaching degree which I now felt was a waste of time and money. Having said that, I am happy I realized it before I graduated from college and was actually working as a teacher.

IT'S OKAY NOT TO KNOW WHAT YOU WANT TO DO AT THIS POINT!

I thought back to what led me to the decision to become a teacher in the first place. I felt silly when I realized that I had not made my career decision by any informed choice, but because I was too afraid of what someone I hardly knew would think about me. Looking back, I should have discussed it with people I knew—with those I loved and trusted. I wish someone had told me it was okay not to know what I wanted to do for the rest of my life when I was barely out of the ninth grade. So I am telling you now.

It is okay not to know what you want to do or how you want to live at this point. You have time to explore all of that. You can take the time to look at all your options.

BUT AGAIN . . . GET TO KNOW YOURSELF

It is truly important that you get to know yourself— your weaknesses as well as your strengths. It is okay to admit that you don't like getting up early in the morning or that you don't want to work for someone else. It is *not* okay to end up in a career that makes you miserable and doesn't fit the kind of life you wish to live. Get clear on exactly what kind of life you do want to live. On the other hand, it is *not* okay to continue to *not* know what you want to do or how you want to live and just float along forever. Life will simply happen to you, instead of you directing and mastering your life.

YOUR INTRODUCTION TO LIFE MAPPING

So, how do you go about discovering what you really would like to do with your life? The answer is, *by designing it.* You may map out exactly the kind of life you think would be perfect for you—the one you may be dreaming of right now—the one in which you would feel the most fulfilled and happy. Everyone deserves a truly wonderful life, and it is what every person hopes for when he or she graduates. The trick is to know how to reach a design conclusion. It's not hard, and I am going to show you how to discover your perfect life. You discover it by asking yourself questions and giving yourself the answers.

Coming up next is an exercise called "Mapping Out your Life." There are spaces left for your answers; however, you may want to put your answers on a separate piece of paper. You will be making some lists and comparing them to each other, and it will be easier if you can lay them side-by-side rather than flipping back and forth in the book. There are no rules for this exercise, but I will ask that while you are doing it, don't limit yourself. While you're dreaming about the life you want to live, dream *big*. Don't hold back! In fact, pretend that money is no issue. You are a millionaire already. You can have anything you want. Just try to get a picture of your highest and best dream life. Anything you want. No matter how silly you may feel in your answer, realize that some part of you desires this. Some part of you would enjoy the things you are dreaming about. Take your time and enjoy the process. Remember, any answer on these pages can be changed at any time. You may simply choose something else.

As you grow, you will change. When something no longer fits for you, you may simply alter it. In each section I will ask questions to stimulate you to fully describe your answers in detail. Read the section first, then just sit back and design your life. Along the way, you may learn some things about yourself that you never knew.

THE LIFE MAP

The Immediate Future

What is your plan when you graduate from high school? Would you like to go on to college or a technical school? Do you hve a job waiting for you after you graduate? Perhaps you are choosing a life in the military. If so, what branch? If you are going on in your education, which college would you like to attend? Why have you selected that particular college? Do you have a course of study or career in mind? If you are in college already, have you chosen a major?

THE LIFE MAP
The Immediate Future

N

In the space below, write your ideas about your immediate future. Use the questions on the previous page as a guide to help you get your thoughts organized.

_____

_____

_____

_____

_____

_____

_____

_____

_____

_____

_____

_____

_____

_____

_____

_____

_____

_____

_____

_____

_____

_____

_____

_____

_____

_____

_____

_____

_____

_____

These questions might seem like they have nothing to do with the perfect life, but you will see as we go along that life is what you're living NOW. The choices you are making at this moment will impact the direction and potential you have to make choices about your perfect life plan. It is where you are today and your starting point. In later chapters you will see why being clear on where you begin will help you plan your perfect life.

Your Perfect Career or Profession

I told you to pretend you are already a millionaire, and because money is no issue, you can just pick the career or work that you think you would enjoy the most. If you could do anything for a living, what would it be? Do you see yourself as a business tycoon heading up some banking system? How about the owner of an exclusive ski lodge somewhere in Colorado? Maybe you would like to be a doctor lending his skills to an underprivileged nation? What service could you provide others? What do you think you would be good at and why? Do you want to work for yourself, or would you like to have an office in your home? Perhaps you would own a building with your office on the top floor. Would you like your place of work to be downtown in some bustling city or out in the suburbs? How many hours a day would you devote to your work?

Your Perfect Career or Profession

In the space below, write your ideas about your perfect career or profession. Use the questions on the previous page as a guide to help you get your thoughts organized.

_____
_____
_____
_____
_____
_____
_____
_____
_____
_____
_____
_____
_____
_____
_____
_____
_____
_____
_____
_____
_____
_____
_____
_____
_____
_____
_____
_____

Look back over your answers. Did you dream big enough? If you elected to work in the city, is it the top floor of some gleaming high-rise, or would you rent space from someone else? If you are driving to work every day, did you consider the cost of a monthly parking garage? If you want to own your own business, did you consider how many employees you will have? If you didn't think any further than the short answer, see if you can go back and flesh out those answers. Think about the details of your career. There are no rules here. If you need to make your answer longer and your plan more detailed, by all means do so.

> *"Cherish your visions and your dreams as they are the children of your soul, the blue prints of your ultimate achievements."*
> *—Napoleon HIll*

Your Dream House and Location

If you could live anywhere in the world, where would you live? Would you live in a city or in a suburb? How about the country? What kind of climate would the area have? Do you enjoy the desert or the mountains? Would you live near water, like a lake or ocean? How about a waterfall? What kind of house would you live in? Would you rather live in an apartment or a townhouse? How about on a farm? What style of furniture would you choose? What color would your rooms be? Describe your bedroom. Would you hire a maid or a gardener? Tell me about the décor. What kind of car or cars would you own?

THE LIFE MAP
Your Dream House and Location

In the space below, write your ideas about your ideal dream house and location. Use the questions on the previous page as a guide to help you get your thoughts organized.

_____

_____

_____

_____

_____

_____

_____

_____

_____

_____

_____

_____

_____

_____

_____

_____

_____

_____

_____

_____

_____

_____

_____

_____

_____

_____

_____

_____

_____

_____

Did you dream in a lot of detail and color? When you answered the question regarding the style of furniture, did you include your artwork? How about the interior of your cars? What would they look like? Leather or cloth? What color is the interior? Go back and write as much detail as you can according to your wants at this particular moment.

The People Who Will Share Your Life

What kind of relationship do you want? Would you like to be single or have a partner? What kind of commitment would you make? A marriage, or would you just explore different relationships? What are you looking for in a partner? Is he or she educated? Is he or she funny? Is the person career-oriented or home-oriented? Is he or she interested in the same things you are, or do you like the idea of opposites to stimulate you to try new things? Will you have children? If so, how many children will you have? Will they go to public school or private school? Will you want to pay for their college expenses, or will you ask them to obtain scholarships? Will you have pets? How many and what kind?

THE LIFE MAP
The People Who Will Share Your Life

In the space below, write your ideas about the people who will share your life. Use the questions on the previous page as a guide to help you get your thoughts organized.

_____

_____

_____

_____

_____

_____

_____

_____

_____

_____

_____

_____

_____

_____

_____

_____

_____

_____

_____

_____

_____

_____

_____

_____

_____

_____

_____

_____

_____

_____

Be careful now. Look back over your answers in the preceding sections. If you said you want to live in an apartment in New York City but want to raise horses, how well are things matching up?

Your Friends and Social Life

Will you entertain a lot in your home? Do you like nights out on the town? What kind of restaurants do you like? Will you have lots of casual friends or just a few really close friends? What kind of people will they be? Will they be educated and busy or artistic and eclectic? Will you give large parties or intimate dinners? Will you live near your family? If not, how often will you go visit them?

Your Friends and Social Life

In the space below, write your ideas about your friends and social life. Use the questions on the previous page as a guide to help you get your thoughts organized.

_____

_____

_____

_____

_____

_____

_____

_____

_____

_____

_____

_____

_____

_____

_____

_____

_____

_____

_____

_____

_____

_____

_____

_____

_____

_____

_____

Relaxation and Hobbies

What kinds of hobbies will you enjoy in your leisure time? Are they indoor hobbies or outdoor hobbies? Will you take regular vacations? Will the whole family go? How will you take care of yourself? How much sleep will you get per night? What kinds of foods will you eat? How about exercise? How often are you outside in the fresh air? Will you schedule regular massages? What kind of clothes will you wear? Are you the formal business-wear type, or are you laid back and casual? Will you visit a salon for your hair and nails? What do you believe in? Will you go to church?

THE LIFE MAP
Relaxation and Hobbies

In the space below, write your ideas about relaxation and hobbies. Use the questions on the previous page as a guide to help you get your thoughts organized.

_____

_____

_____

_____

_____

_____

_____

_____

_____

_____

_____

_____

_____

_____

_____

_____

_____

_____

_____

_____

_____

_____

_____

_____

_____

_____

_____

Adding Meaning To Your Life

What gifts do you think you possess that others could benefit from? What's the one thing you do better than anyone else? Will you share that talent with the world? Do you believe in any cause strongly? If so, would you donate your time and yourself to that cause? How about supporting the cause with your money? What do you hate about the world today? Would you take time to help change that issue? What can you do to "give back" to your community?

In the space below, write your ideas about how you want to add meaning to your life. Use the questions on the previous page as a guide to help you get your thoughts organized.

_____

_____

_____

_____

_____

_____

_____

_____

_____

_____

_____

_____

_____

_____

_____

_____

_____

_____

_____

_____

_____

_____

_____

_____

_____

_____

_____

REVIEW YOUR ANSWERS, BE TRUE TO YOURSELF

Now that you're finished, look back over your answers. Make sure the answers you gave are *your* answers and not what your parents may expect or what your closest friend thinks is right for you. This exercise works best if you are true to your own heart and honest with yourself. If you found that you wrote an answer that is not true to yourself, change it now. For example, if you wrote that you wanted to be a doctor because your mom hopes and dreams you will become one, but you would rather be a clothes designer, then change the answer. This is about *you*. If you think you have to continue golfing as an adult because your dad sees you as the next Tiger Woods, but you hate the sport, then change the answer. Leave golf out of your leisure activities.

> *"I cannot give you the formula for success, but I can give you the formula for failure which is 'Try to please everybody.'"*
> —Herbert Bayard Swoope

This is your dream and your opportunity to say exactly how your most perfect life will look. You don't have to show your answers to anyone. Make sure that you let go of everyone else's expectations for you and answer from your truest self.

BE AWARE OF ANY SUBCONSCIOUS CORE BELIEFS

Once you have gone back and are satisfied that the answers you gave are yours, ask yourself if you dreamed big enough. Sometimes your ideas about yourselves at this stage of your life are warped. By this I mean that you may sometimes believe you are not capable of much when compared to someone else. You may think of yourself as less than you really are. These negative thoughts have a name—subconscious core beliefs.

They are subconscious because they are so engrained in you, you don't even have to think about them to have them rear their ugly heads. They are core because you have bought into them so totally that they now belong to your self-image. I will tell you what to do about them in a later chapter. For now, understand what they are.

Subconscious core beliefs are the monsters that try to force you to limit your potential by undermining your self-worth. *You are and can continue to be limitless in what you can achieve. Recognizing subconscious core beliefs and consciously overriding them is the only way to overcome this roadblock.* Here is an example. If you do not end up valedictorian of your class because you were bored in school and didn't really put in the effort you were capable of, you may not know how capable you are. You may not have tested your capacity to learn. You may now be setting yourself up to think that you are not smart enough or good enough to achieve a grand and wonderful life.

If you would love to learn to surf, but you wouldn't list it as one of your hobbies because you think you don't look good enough in a bathing suit, you have already limited yourself as to what you will enjoy in life. You may look great in a bathing suit, but your subconscious core beliefs are telling you that compared to the models, you're fat.

On the other hand, if it is true that you may need to shed a few pounds and tone up, you have also just eliminated a form of exercise that will work toward the beach body you dream of. Be certain that what you're telling yourself is the truth. Subconscious core beliefs never allow you to change your mind about yourself. The one thing you can be sure of in life is that things will change. You will change, times will change, and everything around you will change. If surfing is one of your secret goals, then by all means go for it.

If you think yourself unworthy, you will live down to that thought and become unworthy. If you think yourself worthy and capable, you will live up to that standard and become worthy and capable in whatever you try. Make sure that none of your answers reflect the idea that you may not be worthy of something greater.

I am going to show you how to effect change in your life so that you can achieve the goals and dreams you have right now. If these goals and dreams happen to change later, that's great. This method still applies to those new goals and dreams. Whatever you want, you can have, if you only see yourself as worthy enough to try achieving your goals.

Look over the Life Map again and see if you limited yourself anywhere because of subconscious core beliefs. If you really wanted to write something down and didn't because the voice in your head told you you're not smart enough to achieve the goal, then you are giving in to subconscious core beliefs. If you heard "I don't deserve that kind of life," then those subconscious core beliefs got you again.

DO NOT LET YOURSELF BE STOPPED BY A MERE THOUGHT

You can easily be your own worst enemy. If you *believe* yourself limitless in your potential, then you will *be* limitless. Don't allow yourself to be stopped by a mere thought. Please be clear about this. You are answering questions about a life that's being designed; it hasn't been lived yet. The object of these exercises is to get you clear on what you really want out of life. You haven't tried to achieve this life and failed, nor have you been rejected by anything or anyone yet. But, you can fail before you begin and you can reject your own dreams of this wonderful life. You can end up living less of your dream than you deserve by limiting yourself now.

You may think that this life plan will begin when you get out of school. I am telling you, it has already begun. It begins with the first ideas you have about yourself. It begins with the first dreams you have for yourself, but stifle, because you think that you are not deserving or capable of achieving them. Get out of your own way!

DO NOT LET ANYONE ELSE STOP YOU EITHER

Every time you hear the negative voice in your head telling you that you can't reach for your dreams, don't listen. Don't allow anyone else to tell you that you aren't capable of achieving them either. One of my favorite quotes comes from Eleanor Roosevelt. She said, "No one can make you less than you are unless you let them."

I knew a girl in high school who dreamed of becoming a doctor. She had a real thirst for knowledge and a passion for the profession. The women's movement was just getting started back then. Women were only beginning to reach for careers that men had dominated up to that point. Her father kept telling her that she should just go to nursing school. He was convinced that his daughter, as a woman, would not be capable of getting through medical school. He also felt that being a doctor would make her less than desirable as a wife, with no time to become a mother.

As old-fashioned as his reasons sound today, he truly felt he was giving his daughter the best advice. She was bombarded with his limiting reasoning every time she brought up the subject. He succeeded in leveling her dreams and she settled for nursing school. She loved working in a hospital environment but was never truly happy in her nursing. Years later, when she was forty, her father passed away. It wasn't until then that she felt free enough to pursue her own wishes. She went back to medical school and became a wonderful surgeon. She is happier than ever and has a wonderful husband and family.

After she became a physician, she told me that she felt she had wasted years of her life by allowing herself to be limited by her dad. She realized that had she not listened to him, she could have been more fulfilled and happier all those years.

I am not saying that you should never listen to what your parents have to say to you. I am not saying that you shouldn't weigh the wisdom of their council. Parents have seen and lived through situations that you have yet to experience. They do have something to offer in the guidance department. What I am saying is that no one but *you* can live your disappointment if you are not happy in your life.

You are the expert of your life. Therefore, it stands to reason that only you will know what will make you the happiest. If you want something badly enough, don't allow anyone to discourage you. It takes planning, compromise, and sometimes several attempts to accomplish a goal, but it can be done. Make sure that your subconscious core beliefs or someone else is not limiting your dream life and the way you design it!

NOW IT'S TIME TO RATE YOUR LIFE DESIGN

Take another look at your answers. Now it's time to go back and rate your life design. I want you to highlight and rate on a scale from one to ten, ten being the highest value, what is most important to you. In other words, if you said you would like to live in the mountains, but also said you like an average temperature of seventy-five degrees, you have a choice to make. You may like the idea of a constant seventy-five degrees; however, the mountains usually experience a wide fluctuation in temperature depending on the season.

If living in the mountains is your strongest pull between those two requirements, then rate this higher than your seventy-five degree temperature wish. If you like the idea of wearing expensive business suits and you don't value a manicure as highly, then rate the clothes higher than the manicure. You don't have to give every answer a rating. You can pick the single most important aspect of a section and not rate any of the others. It is up to you.

I just want you to be clear which of the answers you feel are the most important. Some of them will be vital to you, and some will fall in the category of "wouldn't that be nice." If you find that some of your other answers seem to conflict with the rated ones, it gives you an idea of where you may need to adjust and compromise.

You are beginning to hone your life design down to its finer points. Any life design that you hope to achieve must fit into reality to become real. I don't know of any mountain environment that stays at an average mean temperature of seventy-five degrees. Even in Hawaii, the mountains have temperature variations. You may not be able to have both of those requirements; therefore, the rating will help you know what you can give a bit on and what you need to stand firmly on. You are fitting your dream into the absoluteness of the universe.

DON'T BE AFRAID TO CHANGE YOUR MIND

Designing a life can take a long time to complete, if it ever is complete. It can change at the drop of a hat depending upon how your values change. A life design can be a life long project of achievements and changes. You may live on a mountain and, while vacationing at the beach, decide you like the ocean better. This might lead you to change your plans. Great! Let them change.

Don't be afraid to change your mind. This is what is so terrific about a life map; it can be anything you want and it can change anytime you want. *It is not written in stone; it is written to serve you.* If you need to, go back to the questions often and redo them. It will be interesting to see how you will change and grow as time passes. Your ideas on the perfect life may change and grow with you. You may want to keep these designs in a journal or notebook and look back on them to see how much you have changed. *A life design is not a life sentence; it is a tool you use to gain clarity.*

As much as your life design may change over the years, the constant here is that you will be approaching these changes with a clear idea of who you are and what you want next. If you have clarity about your lifestyle and what you want it to be, then you can set goals to achieve that lifestyle. How awful would it be to drift into a career that anchors you in the middle of some city when you would have been happiest in the country?

When you get this far in designing your life, give yourself a pat on the back. You have already accomplished a great deal; you are on your way to defining exactly what is important to you. Now you can begin putting your efforts toward how you are going to get it!

CHAPTER THREE

Travel Preparation

CHOICES, PERSPECTIVES, AND LUCK

> *"Luck is opportunity met by preparation—and to be prepared*
> *or not prepared is a personal choice.*
> —*Neil Boortz*

BE AWARE OF YOUR CHOICES

In the last chapter you spent a lot of time dreaming about what your life would look like when you were out of school and beginning to live it. I made a statement in the last chapter that bears repeating. You are forming a future life for yourself with the choices you are making at this very moment. *You must be aware of your choices.*

At any given moment, a choice you make may alter your life or the life you have planned for yourself. Choices come in all sizes, shapes, and flavors. Some of your choices may be significant enough as to warrant calling them decisions. These decisions, or big choices, take a lot of thought and consideration.

SO WHAT ARE PERSPECTIVES?

You may even seek the advice of others on the big choices to help you see all sides of the issue. These different sides of the same issue are called perspectives.

Your perspective depends on your view of the subject. If you have ten people in the same room, you can have ten different perspectives. To get an idea of what perspective means, sit on a chair in your bedroom and look at your bed. If I was to ask where your bed was, you could say it's on your right. Now stand on a chair and look at the bed. Since your perspective or view has changed, the location of your bed has also changed in relationship to yourself. Now you would say that the bed is below you on the right. If you stood on your head, the bed would appear to be attached upside-down to the ceiling. As you can see, perspective changes depending on where you stand and how you see something. The definition is the same for ideas or opinions. How you feel about them depends on the angle from which you're viewing them.

When I walk my dogs, I may feel that they need to be unleashed and be able to run freely. If a dog had bitten you at one time or another, you may feel strongly that all dogs need to be leashed. Your view depends upon your experiences and from which side of the dog you view the question. I think that math is a bore but you may love it. Perspectives are neither right nor wrong. Some may seem wrong or contrary to the good of the whole. Entire wars have been fought over perspective. It all depends on the issue. People may view each other's perspectives and try to make them wrong.

> *"You don't get to choose how you're going to die or when. You can decide how you're going to live now."*
> —Joan Baez

They may view them and simply agree to disagree. They may see them as merely another viewpoint. Perspectives are your opinions based on where you stand and what you believe at the time.

I may ask you to listen to one of my perspectives and see if we couldn't come to an agreement on it. It would be your choice to do it or not. So, we have come full circle on perspective and are back at the matter of choice.

Let's start with seemingly small choices—the ones you don't think about much. Let's say that every day when you come home from school you like to have a snack. You usually don't spend the better part of the morning planning what snack you will have that afternoon. Usually the snack choice is made after you have thrown your books on the kitchen table and searched the cupboards for what is available.

Imagine that there are the usual snackable items to pick from. There are fruits, cookies, protein bars, candy, soda, and milk from which you can select or mix and match. Without giving it much thought, you select a candy bar and a soda. Is there a problem with the choice? Not unless it is in complete opposition to what you say you want—unless the snack goes against a goal you have.

UNDERSTANDING HOW CHOICE
AND PERSPECTIVE WORK TOGETHER

This is where choice and perspective work together. Jack is on the wrestling team. His goal for the year is to be state champ in his weight class. He wrestles at 120 pounds and has to make weight on Friday. Today is Wednesday and his weight is 118. He needs to gain two pounds. From Jack's perspective, the extra calories sound like he made the right snack choice.

On the other side is Bob. He also wrestles. His goal is also to be state champ in his weight class. He also wrestles in the 120-weight class and has to make weight on Friday. Today is Wednesday and he weighs 126. He needs to lose six pounds. From Bob's perspective, the same snack choice may keep him from reaching his goal. Notice how these seemingly innocent choices impact the goals that both of these young men have set for themselves. Jack may reach his goal, but Bob may not because he is unaware that the choice he is making now will impact him in the future.

Ellen and Carol both have similar perspectives on how they want their lives to be lived. Both of them are studying international business in college. Their goal is to move to Spain and work in the import/export world. Both have taken the same courses to prepare, except that Ellen has taken three years of French, while Carol has taken three years of Spanish. Which young woman has chosen to prepare to reach her life goal in the best way? In my perspective, Carol is more aware of what she would need to achieve her goal and is better prepared. French will not be of great value or be the best choice in a foreign language for Ellen while she is trying to live and communicate in Spain.

> *"Destiny is not a matter of change, but a matter of choice. It is not a thing to be waited for, it is a thing to be achieved."*
> *—William Jennings Bryan*

Both Bob and Ellen's choices illustrate how you can make poor choices that do not directly support your goals if you do not keep in mind the perspective in which you are making those choices.

MAKE CERTAIN THAT YOUR CHOICES SUPPORT YOUR GOALS

You illustrated your perspective of how you want to live your life in the Life Design exercise. Now, look at the choices you are making at this very moment that will either support or derail those goals. At the same time you are doing this, you will determine whether your perspective and goals for your life will best serve who you are. Let me give you an example of this statement.

Jim and Jane are both trying to decide what they should pursue as careers. Both love the outdoors and are athletic. Both have equal abilities academically. Both are average in math but excel in sciences. Because there is a need for math teachers, Jim has decided to teach math on a high-school level so that he can coach the football team. Jane has decided to go into environmental studies, specializing in fieldwork. According to their hobbies as well as their talents, who do you think has chosen the best field of work? My money goes on Jane.

She has taken note of her strengths, weaknesses, and preferences. She loves being outside. She is better at science than at math. She will most probably excel in her field. She will also probably work in an area of the country that will allow her to enjoy her athletic ability in her leisure time. Jim has zeroed in on his love of athletics and has forgotten that he is just average at math. He has chosen a job that will keep him indoors most of the day to teach something for which he has no passion. While it's true, that Jim will enjoy his coaching, Jane has made the better choice for her all-around fulfillment. Living a truly fulfilled and satisfying life takes the whole of who you are into its perspective—not just one or two areas you may excel in.

HOW TO GET TO KNOW YOURSELF CLEARLY

So how do you come to know yourself clearly? One way is just to notice the choices you have been making so far. Your life is being lived from your perspective, and you will continue to make choices from that perspective. Simply observe and be truthful about what you love to do and what you do well. Be honest about what you don't have a natural inclination toward. Notice your dislikes, and take into consideration what you would like to learn. It all goes into the mix, and you should not ignore any part of it. Luck does not have anything to do with living a great life.

IT'S NOT ABOUT LUCK

We all know people we consider to be lucky. It might be the guy who gets the brand-new, latest-model car for his sixteenth birthday or the girl who gets accepted into an Ivy League school upon graduation. Destiny or fate does not choose one person over another to bless with luck. In fact, I will go so far as to say that the only instance where I would accept the term "luck" is if you win the lottery. The odds are so against any particular set of numbers being drawn; if yours are drawn it is just pure luck.

People make their own luck, and you are as capable of making yours as the next person. Behind each circumstance you consider to be luck will be a whole lot of choices making the certain circumstance happen. The guy who got the new car for his birthday got it because his parents made choices in their life plan that allowed them to prosper enough to afford such a gift to their son. The girl accepted into the Ivy League school gained admission because she chose to make her academic goals high enough to meet the entrance criteria.

There is an old saying that luck favors the prepared. If you wish to receive a certain job, honor, or position, makes it one of your goals. Find out what is required for the job, honor, or position and begin to put your efforts toward fulfilling those requirements.

BACK TO THE SMALLER STEPS

Even if the requirements are so many and look so large that they overwhelm you, chunk them down into smaller pieces. Remember my advice in Chapter 1? Make each step a smaller goal, and then nibble away at the smaller pieces until you have achieved the final large goal. Setting and achieving smaller goals is how you accomplish a huge task. That's exactly what you are doing here.

If you set out to climb Mount Everest, you would not stand at the bottom and in one giant step be at the top. It requires taking hundreds of thousands of steps to reach the summit. It requires preparation and planning to even reach the *bottom* of Mount Everest! It takes learning new skills. The first step is to determine if you would truly like to climb the mountain at all. *This is why I am asking you to get to know yourself—to consciously put effort into combining all your parts together and having a good look at the whole.*

The next exercises are designed to help you look at some aspects of yourself separately so that when you put them together, the picture will be clear. You will start by determining what you were blessed with at birth, or your talents.

YOUR NATURAL TALENTS

On the next page, write ten natural talents you possess today. These ten talents should be things that you do well and that are easy for you or that come naturally to you, like drawing or singing. *Don't let yourself be linear in thinking about talent.* It doesn't always have to fall in the arts or creative section. If you are mechanically inclined and can fix things around the house, then you have a talent. Not everyone can make repairs or even wants to. The running joke around our house is that my husband is allergic to tools. If you put on your makeup or do your hair in such a way that it looks wonderful every day and your girlfriends are always asking you to help them, you have a talent.

If you have a natural bent for sports, which ones are they? How about music? Do you have a natural way with pets or children? What comes naturally to you? Stretch here. Find ten things you feel you do well enough to call them a natural gift or talent. Even if it's a gift for doing yoyo tricks or magic, or working out at the gym, write it down. It may seem small to you now, but I will show you how significant it will become as you zero in on who you are. See if you can fill all ten spaces.

> *"Hide not your talents;
> they for use were made.
> What's a sundial in
> the shade?"*
>
> —*Benjamin Franklin*

MY TEN NATURAL TALENTS

In the space below, write down ten natural talents that you have Use the suggestions on the previous page as guidelines.

1. _____

2. _____

3. _____

4. _____

5. _____

6. _____

7. _____

8. _____

9. _____

10. _____

Excellent! Even if you wrote down three, that's great. All ten would be terrific. You should feel good about this list, no matter how many you filled in. *The fact that you are noticing and are able to realize these natural abilities is a big step.* Some people go through their entire lives and never give themselves credit for their gifts. They judge their talents as insignificant and without merit. Nothing could be farther from the truth.

If you have a natural bent for something, you usually enjoy doing it. If you enjoy doing it, you're usually good at it. Everything that comes easy and natural to you may seem impossible and a challenge to someone else. Because it may be hard for other people to do is exactly why it has value for you.

Everyone has at some point had to learn to tie their shoes; that's why there are no services offering on-the-spot shoe tying. However, even with this example, if you make an unusual bow when you tie your shoes, perhaps you could be the next gift-bow tycoon supplying the world with an unusual and beautiful accessory. The guy who recognized that he had a talent for changing a car's oil quickly could have started the Jiffy Lubes franchise and may now be a millionaire. He knew he had the talent. He didn't minimize it, and he didn't limit himself as to how far he could go. Look at where he went with the idea. He could just as easily have put his talent down and limited himself to one shop in one town and not have maximized his potential.

Take care that you don't put down your own talents and limit yourself. You could be missing out on something really big. In fact, go back and write down those last couple of things you thought were too small or inconsequential to go on your list. Go ahead and own whatever it is you do well. Take credit for what is yours. Don't ever be ashamed or limit your potential. Never hide talent. Rather, you must nurture it and let it find its potential.

YOUR LEARNED SKILLS

Now you are going to make a list of the ten *skills* you possess at the moment. Skills are things that didn't come naturally to you and that you had to learn in order to master them. Few people are born knowing how to add and subtract, type, or do intricate ballet steps. If you have learned to do these things and do them well, list them. Again, don't judge a skill as too small or of too little importance. You never know where these things might lead. *Don't just center your thoughts on school.* If you take dancing lessons after school or practice baseball and have learned the skills it takes to be a good pitcher, write them down. If you took CPR from the Red Cross and find you are really good at this, list it. Open your mind and take credit for your abilities.

MY TEN SKILLS

In the space below, write down ten skills that you had to learn Use the suggestions on the previous pages as guidelines.

1. _____

2. _____

3. _____

4. _____

5. _____

6. _____

7. _____

8. _____

9. _____

10. _____

Good! How many did you manage to write down? Don't feel bad if you have only listed four or five. Skills and learning sometimes depend on how drawn you are to any given thing. Perhaps you just haven't found an area that excites you yet. If you listed ten skills, good for you. No matter how many you have, they all go into your skills bag. Anything you have learned already will also serve you later in life. *There are no small skills—only small thoughts about how important they are.* Any skill you learn is a plus. The more skills you have, the greater your field of choice and ability to excel will be.

If you found that you didn't list a lot of skills, then perhaps you need to get interested in more areas. Broaden your horizons. If there is a course or hobby you think you might like you might, sign up for it.

Lots of girls in my high school took auto shop and not just because there were boys in the class, although I am sure it didn't hurt. Some of them actually wanted to know how to change their own oil and fix their own flat tire if they had to. I don't know how many took it any further and made a life-design decision out of it. However, it sure made them more independent and self-assured.

> *""Life is change. Growth is optional. Choose wisely."*
> *—Karen Kaiser Clark*

Learning skills doesn't always have to point directly at your career goal. Such skills can just be something you would like to have in your "knowledge bag' that may or may not help you out in your career of choice. It sure couldn't hurt. The bonus for gathering skills and trying new things is, the more interested you are, the more interesting you become.

Those girls in shop class had plenty of dates because their interest in changing their car's oil made them more interesting to the guys in their class. No matter what you learn or what you choose to try, learning and trying new things will help you become a more well-rounded person. You will have more to talk about and more to share. You will meet new people with different perspectives about life, and you will make new friends. You will become more at ease meeting new people and trying new things. It's a big world out there and soon you will be moving around in it. Why not get your feet wet now and develop some new skills and have fun while you're doing it?

YOUR HOBBIES

The next list I am going to have you make is your hobbies list. Your hobbies are no less important than your talents and skills. If you take up a particular hobby because you enjoy it, or you have a passion for it, pay close attention to it. Hobbies tell you what you love to do and require no effort or force on your part to participate in them.

You may think that hobbies are just activities for your spare time, but hobbies can figure in a large way into your career. They are also indicators of your preferences and should be weighed as heavily as skills or talents in your life plan. If you have an absolute passion for surfing and it ranks high on your priority list, then plan to live on one of the coasts. If you take a job in Chicago, it's a long walk to the ocean.

You don't always have to give something up to gain something. Your life can be blended in such a way that the design will satisfy many aspects of who you are. Again, I will ask you for ten hobbies. You may not have that many now or ever. Hobbies are choices, too.

Again, be free with your list. Anything you do for pleasure, from singing in the shower to skiing, write it down no matter how far-fetched it may seem. If you enjoy doing it and it's fun, write it down.

Some of the items in your talents list may cross with those in your hobbies list. That's okay. If you have a natural talent for it *and* you pursue it as a hobby, write it down. There will be some crossovers in your lists. If you're a natural dancer and take lessons, consider dancing as a hobby that you like to do, and write it down. Think outside the box. No limiting is allowed.

MY HOBBIES LIST

In the space below, write down ten hobbies that you have. Use the suggestions on the previous page as guidelines.

1. _____

2. _____

3. _____

4. _____

5. _____

6. _____

7. _____

8. _____

9. _____

10. _____

How many did you get? Don't feel bad if there are not exactly ten. You have a lot taking up your time right now, like school and homework. You may not have an overabundance of free time in which to pursue a hobby.

If you're involved in extracurricular activities that you think you can't write down as a hobby, that's okay, too. Just think about them and make sure that you're not overlooking anything. You may not consider student government a hobby, but if you do it because you enjoy it, it is. Not only that, but it is a clue that you may have natural leadership qualities or that you have a passion for politics. *No stone should go unturned.*

You should at least have one hobby for your own relaxation and self-care. One hobby can lead to two hobbies and then three. The point here is that you are doing something you enjoy just for yourself. You are not assigned a hobby in school and you're not doing it for money. Hobbies exist just because you enjoy doing them. Every person should have some hobby that allows him or her the time to relax and enjoy something without any expectations attached to it other than pleasure.

TIME TO REVIEW YOUR LISTS OF TALENTS, SKILLS, AND HOBBIES

If you look back over the last three lists you should begin to get a clear picture of what kind of person you are and what you enjoy doing. You should begin to see a pattern emerge. If you are a natural athlete and you're skilled at baseball, then chances are you will find something on your hobbies list that furthers that. If you love reading and one of your skills is being a speedy reader or having unusual reading-comprehension skills, these will begin to help you define yourself. You should be proud of anything from any of these lists. You may even be shocked by what the lists are showing you.

You may never have thought that you were such an intellectual, but if you're reading a lot, you may be on your way to becoming one. If you love color and take art classes, you may be discovering that you're a creative person. Read your lists again and see how many ways you could describe yourself to someone who can't see you and has never met you. Maybe you thought you weren't particularly interesting, and now you are discovering how interesting you truly are.

Maybe the discovery you are making is that you need to get out more and participate in life. Whatever you find will only help you define and clarify who you are and where you are heading. You may decide that you need to concentrate in one area or on one skill or talent more thoroughly than you have been. You may see that learning another skill could enhance the one you already have. Whatever! Just own everything on these lists. It is all part of who and what you are.

Perhaps this is the first time you have taken time to excavate your true self. Self-discovery is a pleasure, and you will find value in the journey and in yourself. Take pride in it. As you grow, the lists will grow. Update them from time to time and take satisfaction in acknowledging your growth. Remember, you are just starting out in life. Make it a point to sample what life can offer you now. Keep the lists someplace where you can see them easily and add to them occasionally. This will remind you of just how much you are worth and that you are worthy. Even if each list is small, you will find worth when you can add to a list. Challenge yourself. Try something new.

Go back over all three lists. Highlight the talents, skills, and hobbies that are the most important to you. If you have long lists of each, rate them on a scale from one to ten, ten being the highest, according to which is the most important to you—the things that you couldn't live without. If you feel that your life would be diminished if you couldn't use a skill, talent, or hobby, then that skill, talent, or hobby should rank high in your rating.

YOUR STRENGTHS AND WEAKNESSES

Okay, you have come to the last list I will ask you to make for a while. It's a two-column list. The first column will be your strengths and the second will be your weaknesses. You really have to be honest here. You have to look at yourself objectively. You must be real about your weaknesses and proud of your strengths. Humility has its place, but it is not useful when you are trying to get a clear idea of who you are. If you are good at time management, write it down. If you have great organizational tendencies, write that down. Strengths include things like having good leadership skills and sportsmanship. Having an outgoing personality, and being articulate and nonjudgmental—even an optimistic outlook is a strength. Think along these lines while you are listing your strengths.

One the other hand, you will not get a good weakness list if you are in denial. If your room is never clean, it's never clean. List "hates to clean" as a weakness. You cannot dupe yourself into thinking that it could be clean if you just had the time, or that it's messy but you know where everything is. If a clean room were important to you, you would make time to clean it. Besides, it's easy to know where all your stuff is if it's only in one room. No excuses.

A weakness may or may not be a fault. It all depends on how you handle it. First on my list of weaknesses would be getting up in the morning. I cannot seem to do this well. I am unfocused and groggy, off-balance, and sensitive. Grouchy is an understatement; I am no crème puff for the first half hour I am awake. I don't seem to be able to tolerate sound or movement. I certainly can't handle any type of conversation at all.

My worst nightmare is to be confronted with one of those people who wakes up instantly and cheerfully. He or she is ready to greet the day and is actually enthusiastic about what the day might bring. I would love to be one of those people. I am not. I hate the fact that my own children fall all over themselves trying to be the first to leave the kitchen as soon as they see me walk in.

I have tried every form of behavioral modification known to mankind. I tried waking up a half hour early and just not getting out of bed for the first critical half hour. I tried showering in the morning to see if it would bring me around to an alert state faster. It didn't; I felt as if a thousand needles were piercing my tender skin, and it did nothing to improve my mood. I tried going to bed earlier. I even tried a hypnotist. Nothing worked. I can only assume that my body clock and biological rhythms have conspired against me to make me a social disaster in the morning.

The solution I found was to communicate this weakness to my family with honesty and regret and ask them to give me that precious half hour of silence. Because they love me, they have honored my request. Things run smoothly due to their allowance. Getting up in the morning is one of my weakest points. Had I not tried to change the behavior, I would have considered it a fault. I would still try to change it if I thought I could master the task, but it remains something that just is, like a force of nature.

So if you have a weakness that just is, then list it. Only you can determine if it is a fault. If you do determine that it's a fault, give some thought to changing it. Include also on your weakness list anything for which you have a great dislike or unreasonable fear, such as the fear of heights or a dislike for cold weather. If you really don't like snowy, cold weather, you will want to be aware of this before you move to Alaska.

MY LIST OF STRENGTHS AND WEAKNESSES

In the space below, write down ten strengths and weaknesses. Use the suggestions on the previous pages as guidelines.

My Strengths   My Weaknesses

1. _____   1. _____

2. _____   2. _____

3. _____   3. _____

4. _____   4. _____

5. _____   5. _____

6. _____   6. _____

7. _____   7. _____

8. _____   8. _____

9. _____   9. _____

10. _____   10. _____

SORTING OUT THE INFORMATION

Now that the last list is done you can begin to sort out all of this information so that it makes sense to you. If you find that your weakness list is longer than your strengths list, make sure that you haven't been overly critical.

As human beings, it seems to be our tendency to always believe the worst about ourselves and value the best of ourselves too little. Make sure that you have given yourself enough credit for your strengths and that you haven't been too harsh with your weaknesses.

My daughter is an absolute beauty with a figure I can only dream about, yet when she looks in the mirror she sees only what she considers her flaws. She was an honor student in high school but only remembers the one poor mark she made in geometry class. My hope is that, with all the lists you have made, your weakness list does not stand out as all you can see. My fear is that, even with your lists showing your talents, skills, and strengths, you will let this one list outweigh the other three. It shouldn't.

Don't criticize yourself any harder than you would your best friend. Kindness and compassion should be the two gifts you give yourself first. If you don't have them, you can't extend them to anyone else. What you won't allow yourself, you won't allow anyone else either. If you're constantly looking for fault in yourself, it will be easy for you to find fault in others. Who wants a friend like that?

Get all five of your lists together—your life design, your skills and talents, your hobbies, and your strengths and weaknesses. You are going to compare them and cross-reference them to each other to get a clear view of yourself!

N

Λ

CHAPTER FOUR

Plotting Your Course

THE SUM OF YOUR PARTS

"The achievement of your goal is assured the moment you commit yourself to it."
—*Mack R. Douglas*

Now that you have completed your lists and rated them according to your perspective, I am going to show you how to use them to aid you in mapping the best, most perfect life for yourself. If you didn't answer the career section in your life-design sheet because you don't know what you would like to do, you can get an idea of the directions you should explore.

IT'S ALSO GOOD TO KNOW WHAT YOU DON'T WANT

Then again, you may not come up with any defined picture yet, but you may become really clear on what you *don't* want to pursue. Remember my little morning problem in the last chapter? I would not, under any circumstances short of gunpoint, own a bed and breakfast. It would be sheer folly to try to force such a strong weakness to comply with a business that requires me to get up at 5 a.m. and make breakfast for a group of people I don't know. I don't make breakfast for the people I love, let alone some strangers who want their eggs over easy!

Sometimes before you know what you want to do, you are sure of what you *don't* want to do. Knowing what isn't right for you is as valid as knowing what *is* right for you. Any tool that helps you narrow down your choices is useful. This works in any area of your life. If you're looking for a life partner and you don't have a clear idea of what you would like in that partner, but you know that picky eaters are one of your pet peeves, you can be sure you will watch each possible candidate's eating habits. Pay attention to your dislikes.

SEE IF YOU FIND ANY MATCHES ON YOUR LISTS

Start by comparing your lists. You will be looking for anything on one list that matches something on another list. For example, if you said on your life-design sheet that you would love to live in Colorado, and on your skills list you stated that you are good at skiing, that is a match. If skiing also appears on your hobby list, you can be pretty sure you are on the right track. That's a complete match. See how many matches you can make between your skills, talents, hobbies, and strengths and weaknesses lists and your life-design sheet.

There may also be things that, although they may not match exactly, will support something on another list. If you said that you loved being outdoors and enjoyed athletics,

> *"Great things are not done by impulse, but by a series of small things brought together."*
> —*Vincent Van Gogh*

that would support a decision to live in the country. If you have already chosen a career or profession, the other lists should support your choice. It doesn't need to be a total and perfect matching of everything on each list, but certainly the majority should be in alignment. If you find things out of alignment, think about how you can compromise them to fit them into your overall plan. Check their rating; perhaps you rated these things so low that you can even do without them.

LET YOUR LISTS GUIDE YOU

If you don't know what you want to pursue as a career yet, let the lists guide you. Look at all your skills, talents, and hobbies. See if a common thread emerges. These common threads tell you that you are leaning toward a preference. It's much easier to be fulfilled in a life's work for which you have a passion than to grind out your life working at a job you don't enjoy. It's much easier to greet each day happy to do your work rather than spend years on a countdown to retirement. Don't wish your life away. Rather, enjoy each moment of it.

Clarity on the emerging threads or preferences you have at this moment is a great start. Suppose it says on your hobby list that you enjoy photography, and on your skills list you stated that you took a photography class to learn how to properly use the f stop feature on your camera. On your talents list you wrote that you were artistic. You may want to explore those three features and look at career opportunities that allow you to use those elements. Newspaper photography, art that uses photography as a medium, film school, portrait or landscape photography, or commercial photography are some examples of career opportunities. If you happened to have listed flying as a hobby, then add it to the mix and consider aerial mapping by photography as a possibility.

The point here is to find as many possibilities that match what and who you are already. Film school may be a reach away from still photography, but those skills can be learned. You can go to school to refine and perfect your craft. You cannot as easily fit what you are *not* into a life's work. Research potential careers on the Internet, or at this point you may want to enlist the aid of a parent or close friend to go over your lists with you. They may have knowledge of a career that you don't even know about yet.

Don't ignore your weaknesses or dislikes. If you are looking at a list like the one above and you see that you don't really want to work for someone else, then scratch off newspaper photography. If you hate to fly, do the same with the aerial-mapping idea. All of these lists will help you define what you really want out of your life and at the same time will help you become clear on what elements you *don't* want in your life.

WHAT TO DO WHEN YOU FIND DISCREPANCIES ON YOUR LIST

You may find some glaring discrepancies on your list. You may have listed in your lifestyle section that you would love to live in a two-story colonial home with a large grassy yard shaded by huge oak trees for your children to play in. You may also have listed Phoenix, Arizona, as the section of the country where you would like to live. You then have some choices to make. Phoenix is an arid, hot region that does not lend itself to lush lawns or large shady oak trees. It can be done, but it requires lots of maintenance. Is that what you want? Would you like to spend your weekends maintaining your lush lawn? Perhaps you would rather spend your weekends traveling, which you also may have included on your list. Here is where the rating system plays a large part.

If you rated living in Phoenix higher than the house and the yard, then rethink your housing style. Something closer to the native architectural style may do just as well. If the house and yard are musts, find out where large oak trees and colonial homes are plentiful and natural.

When you do run across discrepancies, don't forget your creativity. Design your life to fit what you want.

Perhaps you share my weakness for not liking to get up in the morning, and you don't want to work for anyone else—but yet your dream has always been to own a bed and breakfast. Get creative! Don't let the idea of a bed and breakfasts limit you. The only things limiting you are the boundaries you impose on yourself. Learn to look at each idea or problem from as many perspectives as you can. There are many solutions to a problem, and the more perspectives you can see, the more choices you have to choose from. You could redesign that career; tailor it to fit your wants and needs. Evolve the breakfast venue into a bed and brunch, or a bed and dinner. Sounds great to me! I would be your first customer, and I am sure there are hundreds of others out there like me who like to sleep late and would appreciate the later meal.

YOU CAN ALWAYS CHANGE YOUR LIFE MAP

If you have made any startling discoveries, or your lists don't match the life you have designed for yourself, you may want to go back and make some changes in the life-design sheet. Perhaps after seeing what skills you have and what hobbies you prefer, your original choice doesn't seem appealing to you. By all means, change it. The whole point of these exercises is to really look at what you have already planned and see if it fits who you are at the moment. Does it support what you want out of your life? If what you're planning doesn't seem to fit with who you are, make another choice. You can do that.

"If you live without feeling the need to change or have courage to make the change then you merely exist."
—Brandon Abernathy

If you make a poor choice, don't stick with it because you think you have to. The good news is, *you can always choose again.* Even if you feel you have made a mistake and you're already down one road of choice, at any time, you can simply choose again. By taking these steps now and becoming clear on your best life, you are avoiding the possibility of graduating from school and entering a life that will make you miserable. Imagine how disheartened and depressed you would be if you felt you were doomed to living out your entire life in a situation you didn't like.

True, if that were to happen you could always choose again, switch careers, or go back to school and prepare for another career. But why waste the time and money when you can get clear now?

WHAT IF YOU ENJOY A LOT OF THINGS

You may also find that you have many interests and that you enjoy a lot of different activities. You may feel a sense of frustration at having so much choice that you can't decide what to pick. That's terrific; don't let that problem frustrate you. As you grow and get farther along in your studies and your life, a definite pattern will emerge. You will begin to lean more heavily toward one field than another. Just keep your lists up-to-date, and you can be sure you will begin to branch off more heavily in one area than another.

THE MONEY FACTOR

You may experience something else as you go along in this quest of self. You may begin to feel you are picking careers because you are sure they will make you a lot of money. It may seem as if you don't care much about any of the other lists as long as you end up rich. You may also fear that what your lists show you're interested in won't make as much money as, say, a doctor or lawyer. Money and living well are natural goals that drive us all. Who would choose to be poor? We all want a great life with all the little trimmings that make it fun and luxurious. There's no shame in this. The shame would be living a life that does not suit you solely for the money.

Say you choose to become a doctor because you assume you can make yourself wealthy. You choose becoming a doctor even though you don't particularly like dealing with people on a regular basis. You're kind of shy and you hate the sight of blood. To dedicate your life to this profession would make you miserable, and you would probably make a lousy doctor. If you're miserable, and you're a bad doctor, word will get around. No one wants to be the patient of a doctor who is grouchy or who faints if stitches are needed. Fainting doesn't instill a lot of confidence in your patients. You may end up with a light patient load and not make the big bucks you had hoped for. And you may hate what you do as well.

Money is a currency, but there are more currencies than money in life. Money is just *one* currency. Happiness is also a currency; so is love. Anything you would strive to do or have in your life can be a currency to you. If you love playing your video games, but your mother won't let you play them unless your room is cleaned every week, you will clean your room so that you can play those games. Video games are one of your currencies.

> "The only limits in us are the ones we set on ourselves."
> —Manuel Careasquillo

Mary may have five currencies she values in her life, while David may have just three. How many currencies a person may have is individual to each person. I know you have heard this before, but money cannot buy happiness. It can make you physically comfortable while you are mentally miserable, but what a trade-off. Don't sacrifice yourself for the sake of a big paycheck. You don't have to.

Don't fear that just because you would love to make ice cream for your life's work, you won't make enough money to live the good life. Ben and Jerry have no trouble paying their bills.

POTENTIAL AND POSSIBILITY

Here is what makes money—finding what you are good at doing, what you would love to do, and what you have a passion for, and then thinking big. Do not limit yourself to just one ice-cream stand, but go for a chain all over the country. If you find your career niche in life, and it's a passion of yours, allow yourself to explore the limits of where that career can go. If you then set your goals to get there, you will be successful. You will enjoy what you do and will look forward to working. Your passion for your work will drive you to expand your horizons and take your life to its full potential. In the meantime, while you're discovering what this passion is, be encouraged that you want to live life in a large way. That's called drive. Armed with the right tools, along with drive, you will be pointed in the right direction, and your life will become all potential and possibility.

N

CHAPTER FIVE

Getting Directions

BEGIN TO CREATE YOUR PERFECT LIFE NOW

> *"Personal power is the ability to take action."*
> *—Anthony Robbins*

Now that you have finished all your lists, you should be gaining some sort of general clarity on what kind of person you are and what type of work you would like to do. If you gained clarity on what kinds of work you would *not* like to do, that is just as valid. At least an awareness of what you like and don't like is beginning to form in your head.

You are also starting to see your skills and talents as potentially useful in your life. Your lists are likely to weigh more heavily in one area than in another. Your lists may point out that most of the activities you participate in and enjoy are done outside. You then know to research careers that will include working outside more than sitting behind a desk. On the other hand, if you see your emerging threads telling you that your time is spent in the library or behind a computer, don't explore the idea of becoming an outdoor adventure guide.

MAKE ACTIVE CHOICES RIGHT NOW

You may think at this point that you are done with your life design and that you can sit back and wait until you are out of school for the perfect life to begin. Not true—it has begun already.

There is no such thing as stumbling into your perfect life. It does not drop out of the sky on you at the point of graduation. Even if others tell you that they consider themselves the luckiest people in the world for chancing upon their perfect career, life, marriage, or home, they are not revealing the total picture. If you question them, you will find that when opportunity knocked, they were there to answer it at the right time, with the right tools, and in the right frame of mind to accept that potentially perfect life. What you will find is that at certain times in their lives, they made active choices that led them to where they are today. Where they give luck the credit, the choices came from following their heart's calling and becoming skilled at it.

> *"No dream comes true until you wake up and go to work."*
> *—Unknown*

There is no such thing as starting too soon. There is, unfortunately, such a thing as coming to the realization that you denied your calling, chose a field of work you weren't really interested in or suited for, and regretted it later. You can start too late. Right now is the time when you should be aware that choice is critical in your life. Let me say this again. *What you choose right now, at this moment, is critical to obtaining your perfect life.* It can be the seemingly small choices that can alter your future. Pay attention to the choices you make. You cannot start too soon.

There are plenty of professional athletes who began playing their sport when they were four, five, and six years of age. Because they enjoyed it so much, they made time in their lives to play all the time. They played little league or junior hockey. They played flag football before they ever thought about tackling anyone. They were knocking a golf ball around the backyard before they even got a look at a real golf course. But they had a passion for it.

They continued that passion into extracurricular activities in their school years and became proficient at it. They learned the rules of the game and conditioned their bodies for it. Yes, there were some who had a real natural gift for their sport, but there were others who worked at it one step at a time until they, too, became an expert. They worked at it because they wanted to play the sport, and they wanted to play because they loved it and had a passion for it. The Tiger Woods and Wayne Gretskys of the world made a conscious choice at some point in their lives as to how they wanted to live their lives. They designed their most perfect lives. Then they held the picture in front of them for the years it took to meet their long-range goals. They planned and perfected the skills they would need to make that perfect life happen. They didn't start too late—four or five years old wasn't too soon.

If you graduate from high school never having played football and expect a full football scholarship from the Nebraska Cornhuskers, you are going to be disappointed. If you dream of being lead guitarist in a rock band that you will put together with your high-school friends who share that dream, yet you don't play guitar, how well do you think your plan will work? If you started taking guitar lessons in junior high school or earlier, and you practiced and perfected your guitar playing every day, you may have the skills. Perhaps while moving in that circle of musicians and teachers, you came across like-minded individuals who were also perfecting and practicing their instruments. If under these circumstances, you form a group, you may have a good chance of obtaining your dream.

BE SURE TO PREPARE AND PLAN

The point here is, don't expect to grab the brass ring if you don't prepare and plan. It will not happen. You won't be there at the right time in the right place with the right skills to take advantage of the opportunity. There is no such thing as "too soon" to start thinking about your life and making some long-range goals.

BE REALISTIC IN YOUR EXPECTATIONS
AND DON'T LOOK JUST FOR FAME

When choosing those long-range goals remember to be realistic in your expectations. We all have dreams of fame. They may all take different forms. Joe might dream of being the star quarterback of a top NFL football team, while Steve may dream of singing in front of thousands of screaming fans. We yearn to be recognized and held in esteem, even worshipped. Most of us place this yearning into the dream of becoming a professional athlete, a rock star, or a movie star because it is the first most visible form of fame that we recognize in our youth. When we finally come to the realization that we aren't led in the direction of sports, music, or drama, we begin to look for other ways of gaining recognition and abundance for our chosen fields.

> *"My friend, if I could give you one thing, I would wish for you the ability to see yourself as others see you. Then you would realize what a truly special person you are."*
> —B.A. Billingsley

I knew math majors in college who formed an Einstein Club because they held Einstein in such high esteem. They loved math and the creativity—yes, I said creativity—of math as their passion. Personally I don't see it; I am not good at math. If I run out of fingers and toes I am lost. But math didn't have to be my passion or my dream to appreciate the excitement with which those math majors approached their field. Just to see people excited and passionate about their chosen field enthused me. It made me long for a career that I, too, could feel inspired about.

The yearning you feel for recognition and fame is coming from the deepest part of you. It is your potential screaming to be fully utilized. I truly believe that each of us enters life with a gift that belongs solely to us. We are all gifted with an area of brilliance, or a genius. This gift is something you can do better than anyone else, and its potential is meant to be shared with the rest of mankind. When you are young and feel your gift begin to scream out to be fully expressed, you may mistakenly attach those feelings to the things that are the most popular or most visible signs of brilliance. This would be athletics, music and film.

Not all of us are meant for greatness in those fields, but *we all are meant for greatness.* That greatness lies inside each of us, just waiting to be discovered and developed. Don't try to force yourself to be anything other than what you are for the sake of fame. The most wonderful thing you can be is just who you are, and the most wonderful way of obtaining your perfect life is to be aware and to live the awareness. That awareness begins with your lists, your self-discovery. If you are true to yourself and live your potential, then fame will take care of itself.

START SETTING SHORT-RANGE GOALS

The first step is to start using the potential you have discovered in yourself to its fullest. So ask yourself the following question. What am I doing at this moment to prepare to use my gift to its fullest potential? Am I setting short-range goals that will support and help me achieve the long-range goals I have determined will make me the happiest in my life?

If on your life-design list you came up with what you feel is the single most wonderful choice for your career, then that's great. You now have direction. You can begin to set short-range goals that will support your life choice. These choices will be made with that long-range goal in mind. The short-range goals are steps to obtaining your long-range goal. As Dr. Martin Luther King Jr. said, "Keep your eyes on the prize."

Before you proceed with goal setting and with how you break down goals into manageable pieces, I want to remind you again of the flexibility of these choices. Be aware that you can change your mind. Be open to this. If the choice you have made suddenly doesn't work for you anymore, choose again. If you are like the majority of us, there will be three or four careers you may see yourself in. You may not be prepared to make the decision to concentrate on just one area yet. That's okay, too. Here is how you proceed from this point no matter which of the above statements may apply to you.

TRY TO EXPERIMENT ON A SMALL SCALE
WHAT YOU MAY WANT FOR YOUR CAREER

Let's say that you have decided you want to be a veterinarian or that a veterinarian is one of the possible choices you have listed. What you are striving to do is narrow down the choices in order for you to be absolutely sure that being a vet is what you want to devote your life to. What can you do at this moment to be sure?

Call your local veterinarian and tell him or her about your ambition. Explain to the veterinarian that you have either chosen this field or that you are thinking about it as a possible choice. Ask if the veterinarian has a program that allows you to work with him or her for a period of time and observe the day-to-day life, lived by a veterinarian. If he there isn't a program, suggest that you might be willing to volunteer to exercise the animals that are boarding at the clinic right now. Ask about summer employment. Chances are good that you can perform some task or service for the veterinarian, allowing you to observe and learn what really goes on in the field you are choosing.

While you are there, don't limit your conversation to just the veterinarian. Speak with the receptionist and the veterinary assistant. Look at it from all perspectives. Each person in that office will have his or her own opinions. If for some reason it is impossible for you to get into the veterinarian's office, call another office and try again. Use your resources. If your mother's sister's husband golfs with a veterinarian on Saturday afternoons, ask your mother to talk to her sister to get her husband to speak to the veterinarian for you. If there is just no way to get into a veterinarian's office, try an animal groomer or look for summer work on a farm—anything that will get you around animals.

When my daughter was in seventh grade, she thought she might like to be a veterinarian. It was something she was considering as one of her long-range goals. She had a passion for animals and wondered if she would be happy as a veterinarian. One day while taking our little dog for her annual shots, I posed the question of allowing her to come in and do some odd jobs for the veterinarian on weekends so that she could get a first-hand look. I also asked if he might be able to tell her the classes she would need to concentrate on now, as well as how much schooling she could expect to have to take. He whole heartedly agreed to my idea.

Things went along great for the first couple of weekends. She walked dogs, filled water dishes, and even got to observe the veterinarian while he met with the owners of his patients. She had the opportunity to see a litter of puppies being born and watched while he stitched up a cat that had been involved in a fight. She loved it. Everything she saw convinced her that she would love doctoring animals and helping them get over their aches and pains. Everything was great until the fifth weekend.

She was observing the veterinarian when an elderly woman brought in the most ancient dog in the world. It was a small mixed-breed dog—nothing special but dearly loved by the woman. The old dog and the woman had lived together for many years, and the dog was her company and comfort after she lost her husband. The poor dog was suffering from old age. It could hardly walk, and because it was overweight, it was suffering from diabetes that had now gotten to the critical stage. There was nothing the veterinarian could do to ease the dog's pain. The only thing left was to put

"If opportunity doesn't knock, build a door.
—Milton Berle

the animal down. As you can imagine, the woman was terribly grieved by the news that her dear friend would have to be put to sleep. My daughter was horrified. When the old woman began to cry, my daughter also began to cry and had to leave the room. In fact, it affected my daughter to the point that she called me to pick her up earlier than we had scheduled. She cried for days every time she thought about it. She told me that if she had been in the veterinarian's place, she could never have put the old dog down. Because of this, she didn't feel she could ever come to terms with this part of being a veterinarian. At that point, she crossed the possible career off her list. She still loves animals today and has a natural way with them, but she discovered that she did not want all the tasks associated with being a veterinarian.

Although it was a sad way to learn what she didn't want or couldn't do, it was much better to have experienced it at that point of her life. She did not assume out of ignorance that she would love the career and spend years in veterinarian school. She would have ultimately been disappointed and heartbroken.

This example illustrates the importance of trying to find a way to experience, on a small scale, what you think you may devote your life to. It may turn out to be the perfect choice for you, or, like my daughter, you may find out that one small part of the choice is something you wouldn't want to experience on a regular basis.

OTHER WAYS OF RESEARCHING CAREERS

If by some twist of fate you cannot find someone close to you in the field you would like to sample, there are other ways of researching. Get on the Internet, go to the library, ask your guidance counselor, or read someone's biography. Write a university that offers that course of study and ask for a class list of what you would be taking should you pursue the field. Check it over and see if you are interested in the types of classes required for that degree. If the field you're researching is more on a vocational level, find out which technical schools offer the training. If there is a college or technical school in your area, visit it and ask if someone could refer you to a student in the area of study. Talk to the student and ask questions. Find out what goals he or she is developing and what direction the student wants his or her life to take.

Whatever you're considering as a career, whether it is one choice or several, most schools, even high schools, have elective courses to help you experience what you're considering. If you think you would like to be an auto mechanic, then take courses pertaining to mechanics as electives. If science is your thing, then take all the extra or advanced sciences available to you. Join the environmental club. If your school doesn't offer your interest as an elective—say, for example dance—then find a school of dance in your area and take a couple of classes in your after-school hours. If you want to become a chef, work in a restaurant to get the feel of the lifestyle and take any cooking classes offered in your community. Do whatever it takes to help you refine your goals and become more definite in your choices.

INVEST IN YOUR LIFE—INCLUDING YOUR EDUCATION

No matter what you plan on pursuing, more than likely it will take more specialized training than you can receive in high school. You will have to do some form of study or internship after you are out of school to really hone in and become proficient at your chosen career. The majority of these specialty schools, and most definitely colleges, have certain standards for admission. They will want to know before they admit you to their school that you are serious about learning and not just taking up a space. That begs the next question. How are your grades?

The worst thing you can do for yourself at this moment is not being invested in your life. Right now your life includes school. If you think school is a bore and strictly a social event and you are making poor grades, you are cheating yourself out of living your dream life. The education you are getting now is the single most important aspect of preparing you for the opportunity to live a great life. In the event you are attending a private secondary school and you're still not taking your education seriously, then shame on you for wasting your parents money.

By far the most popular complaint of young people today is that their parents and teachers treat them like little children. Well, if you walk like a duck and talk like a duck, everyone is going to treat you like a duck. If you wish to be treated with the respect of a young adult and be afforded the freedom of a young adult, then show us a young adult.

BE RESPONSIBLE AND ACCOUNTABLE FOR YOUR ACTIONS

It is important that you take responsibility for your life and being accountable for your actions. Take the world you live in now seriously. Your career now is to get yourself an education that allows you to continue on to college or technical school and that prepares you for living independently. No parents in their right mind will ever say to you, "Hey you're doing poorly in school, which means you are not mature enough to realize how important this time of your life is. You spend your time playing pool or hanging with your friends, and I have heard rumors you may be drinking regularly. Go ahead and take charge of your life and, oh by the way, here are the car keys." If this explanation escapes you, let me try to help you understand with an example a little closer to home.

Your friend Karen admires your taste and loves the way you dress. She borrows your clothes on a regular basis, but when she returns them, they are wrinkled and smell of cigarette smoke. Several times there have been burns or rips in them. Karen still has a couple of your sweaters that she borrowed

> *"The price of greatness is responsibility."*
> *—Winston Churchill*

last winter and there is no indication she will ever return them. How do you feel about lending Karen your clothes? I can almost guarantee that she wouldn't be borrowing more of my clothes. Now if Karen had taken responsibility for my clothes and had been accountable for their condition, and if she had returned them clean and in the same good shape in a reasonable amount of time, she may still have the privilege of picking from my closet. She would be accountable for her action of borrowing and taking responsibility for it. The same goes for your parents.

If you demonstrate to adults that you don't know or accept the first ideas about responsibility and accountability, you won't be treated as a young adult. The best thing you can do to illustrate to your parents and teachers that you want more control over your life now is to take life seriously.

A large part of taking your life seriously is to be really clear that your education is preparing you to be financially and emotionally independent. Be responsible for investing yourself in that preparation. Be clear by choosing to pay attention to the details of your life today, tomorrow, and every day. Your long-range goal is to be skilled enough to further your education when the time comes. Your short-term goals should be centered every single day on what you can do to achieve your long-range goal. You cannot start achieving those short-range goals too soon. In the meantime, you will be earning the respect of your parents and teachers and gaining more control over your life. That's killing several birds with the same stone.

TRY TO COMMUNICATE WITH YOUR PARENTS

On the other hand, if you are making great grades and are receiving good reports about your conduct in school, and you feel your parents are still overly strict with you, try sitting down and really communicating your feelings to them. Explain to them that you feel your actions are showing an awareness of responsibility and accountability, and see if you can negotiate a solution that suits you both.

I know some parents whose children make wonderful grades and are very responsible, and the parents are still very strict with them. Remember, along with hoping that you will achieve everything you want out of life, your parents are coping with fears of their own. Safety is a huge issue with parents. They also fear that if they loosen the grip on you, you will feel like you don't have to study or make the grades anymore. Silly? Well, maybe. A case can be made for either side of that issue. Just don't expect your parents to give up all the control in one day. Negotiate small steps, and as they see you can handle your independence in a good way, you can negotiate for more. Don't even bother trying the screaming and demanding route. It won't work.

* * *

Now that we have talked about your responsibility to your education and have hopefully gotten clear on what long-range and short-range goals can help you accomplish in your schoolwork, let's begin to understand how to chunk down those goals into doable pieces.

If you're making an F in science and would like to set a goal that by the next grading period you will make at least a C, and this looks overwhelming to you, let me show you how to chunk down that goal into pieces that you can work on everyday.

> *"The reason most people never reach their goals is that they don't define them, learn about them, or even seriously consider them as believable or achievable. Winners can tell you where they are going, what they plan to do along the way, and who will be sharing the adventure with them.*
> —Denis Waitley

N

CHAPTER SIX

One Mile At A Time

CHUNKING DOWN YOUR GOALS

> *"Failing to prepare is preparing to fail."*
> *—John Wooden*

A goal is a standard or achievement you haven't met yet. If you had already met that standard, then it would be called an achievement or accomplishment, not a goal. Whether you are aware of it or not, you set a lot of goals for yourself in the course of a day. They can be as small as getting yourself to school in the morning on time.

SET UP A STRUCTURE FOR WHAT YOU NEED TO ACCOMPLISH

A goal is preceded by the awareness that you must accomplish a task; in the case of getting to school, you became aware that you need to be on time. The next step you take is setting up a structure that includes all the things you need to accomplish before you can leave the house. This structure is chunked down into small steps that allot an amount of time in which each step needs to be completed so that your time deadline for leaving the house can be met.

Bill may set his alarm for only an hour before he needs to meet his time goal because he can prepare for leaving quickly. Judy may have to set her alarm for two hours before leaving because she requires more time to accomplish the steps she has in her preparation structure. Where Bill may just comb his hair, Judy will need extra time to use her curling iron and put on her makeup. Each of them has the awareness of the preparation they want to make to leave and can set their alarm clocks to accomplish their goals. Notice there is a thought process that goes on here, however conscious or unconscious it may be.

BE AWARE OF YOUR CHOICES

You are making small choices that lead to larger goals all the time. *It is being aware that you are making those choices, and knowing what those choices are, that are the keys to success.* There is rarely only one choice you can make to achieve the same goal. Being aware that you are choosing allows you the opportunity to decide which choice can lead to your goal in a better, more efficient manner.

SEPARATE YOUR GOALS INTO STEPS AND TIME LIMITS

As you read before, there are steps that follow these choices. These steps are little chunks of action that need to be taken in order to achieve the goal. When you separate any goal into steps, it's called chunking. Chunking down an overwhelming task makes it much easier to achieve. Making a list of the chunks you have determined need to be accomplished before you can reach your goal is an excellent way to track your progress. Each time you accomplish a chunk, cross it off your list. Lists also help you keep on task.

Some people are natural chunkers; others must learn how to do this. Mothers practice chunking and goal setting every day. They have to in order to be efficient and get things done. If your mom has to grocery shop, drop off the cleaning, and pick up your sister from kindergarten, she chunks those goals down into smaller steps in order to accomplish them in an efficient manner. She doesn't go to the grocery store and come home, put all the groceries away, and then go back out to drop off the cleaning, come home, and then go back out once again to pick up your sister. Rather, she plans to go out a specified amount of time ahead of the deadline to pick up your sister and completes her tasks one after the other, leaving enough time to reach the school when your sister walks out the door. Many little choices and decisions went into chunking down her plan.

Let's go back to the F in science. When you first open your report card and see that F, you can choose to do one of three things. One, you can choose to do nothing (disclaim responsibility). Two, you can choose to blame someone else. You did everything right, but the teacher doesn't like you so she didn't mark you fairly (refusing to be accountable for your actions). Or three, you can choose to do something about the grade (accepting both responsibility and accountability for your actions).

You can make the first choice of doing nothing—not advisable, but again, your choice. If this is the case, then no other action need be taken. Suppose you choose choice two. Blaming is useless and is the best way to demonstrate that you have no accountability for your actions. You will show that you have no control over your life and not willing to accept any. It's always someone else who does something or makes you do something that leads to a bad result. It's also boring. So let's eliminate that one. In choice three you are making the decision to set a goal to improve the situation.

BEGIN WITH WHAT IS

There are steps that will help you improve your grade even if it looks overwhelming at first glance. *You begin with what is.* You have an F in science, and you are choosing to work on getting a different result. The different result is at least a C in science. What happens between those statements is a lot of chunking down and achieving smaller goals within a time limit. You want the grade improved by the next grading period.

DETERMINE YOUR POSSIBILITIES

Now you need to decide what steps you must take to improve the grade. What are the possibilities? Perhaps doing the homework and turning it in on time would help. How about asking the teacher for extra help after school? Maybe you have a friend who excels in science and could come over after school and explain it to you in such a way that your understanding will be greater.

> *"How do you eat an elephant? One bite at a time."*
> —Unknown

CHOOSE A ROUTE, OR SEVERAL ROUTES, TO ACHIEVE YOUR GOAL

You must look at those possibilities and choose a route, or several routes if necessary, depending on how strongly you are committed to your goal. Doing your homework requires two steps of its own. The first step in the homework choice is physically sitting down and doing the homework no matter what. Step two is actually turning it in on time the next day. You may have to sacrifice your favorite TV program in order to do this one. Not very appealing, but the choice works toward your goal. Your list might look like this.

1. 4:30—do science homework and put in notebook
2. 7th period—turn homework in to teacher

The second choice is to ask the teacher for some extra tutoring after school. Chunk this task down into steps. First arrange to stay after class one day to talk to the science teacher. Once you have done that, move on to chunk two. Assuming the teacher says yes, arrange and assign a time every day you will meet. Chunk three would be arranging your schedule to keep your appointment with the teacher and be on time. In this step you may also have to arrange a ride home after your tutoring. Just three chunks and you have accomplished the tutoring goal. Your list may look like this.

1. Arrange to stay after school on Tuesday and talk to Mr. Jones
2. Arrange with Mr. Jones, date and time for tutoring
3. Reschedule any activities on tutoring days and get a ride home from school

The third choice could be chunked down the same way, arranging the time and day and being committed to showing up and showing up on time. Now you choose which method you feel will serve you best, or choose all three if you are super committed to making the grade goal within your timeline.

Every time you make a commitment, set a smaller goal, and achieve it, you are well on your way to achieving the larger original goal. Before you know it, you have achieved all the chunking down steps and have managed to reach your original goal of bringing your grade up to a C.

In your life-design exercise you have set the large goal of living the perfect life. There are a lot of smaller goals that must be met contained within the framework of larger goals. Some are long-range, and others you will be setting for yourself in the present moment.

Living the perfect life means living where you want to live and doing what you most want to do, with whom you want to do it. It means having a certain type of house with a certain color bedroom and driving a

> *"True genius lies not in doing extraordinary things, but in doing ordinary things extraordinarily well."*
> *—Unknown*

certain model car. All of these smaller conditions or goals must be met in order for you to achieve the large goal of the perfect life. All of these smaller conditions, chunked down from the large goal, can also be chunked down and achieved in the same manner you chunked down the science grade.

PAY ATTENTION TO THE DETAILS OF YOUR LIFE

In fact, although it may seem like a small thing to you at the moment, your science grade may have a direct impact on whether or not you get to live your dream life. Pay attention to the details of your life. Understand that you are making decisions and setting goals for yourself <u>right</u> <u>now</u> that will lead to achieving or not achieving the perfect life.

PRACTICE, PRACTICE, PRACTICE

The more you consciously practice the process of goal-setting and chunking down, the easier and more natural it will become for you. Try it on things that are seemingly without thought. Next time you would like a soda, practice goal-setting and chunking.

Your goal is the soda, and the chunking are the steps and small goals you need to accomplish to obtain the soda. Have the following conversation with yourself: "I would love a soda; it is my immediate goal to get that drink for myself. To reach the soda, I must chunk down the goal. My first chunk is to get up off the couch and go to the kitchen. Done. Second step is to open the refrigerator and get the soda out. Done. Third step is to twist the cap off the bottle. Done. Fourth step is to drink it. Done. Larger goal accomplished!" This may seem like a small thing, but the more you practice and understand, the more aware you will become of choice and goal-setting. When the bigger goals come up, it will be easy for you because you practiced.

A CHALLENGE FOR YOU

Getting the soda was easy; everything else you want for yourself can be accomplished just this simply. *Don't ever let the size of your goal scare you.* It is just a bunch of little steps and smaller goals to be accomplished. They may look large, but you have just learned how to scale them down to a manageable size and accomplish them.

Now that you have perfected the "getting the soda" goal, I am going to invite you to take on this challenge. Pick out three goals for yourself. The first should be relatively short-range. Choose a goal you can accomplish in a day. How about something simple like cleaning your room? Unless you feel you need to rent a backhoe to shovel things out first, you should be able to accomplish this in one day.

Next pick a goal that can be accomplished in a week. The third goal should be something you feel you can accomplish in a month. Practice chunking down each goal by making lists for yourself about the natural sequence of steps you will have to go through to reach each goal. There may be smaller goals you need to meet to support the larger goal before the larger is achieved.

Please make an effort to list goals that require something of you. Don't list "waking up" as your one-day goal. Although it beats the alternative, it hardly requires much conscious effort on your part.

I am asking you to start with really short-range goals for another reason. Along with practicing your methods of achieving goals, each time you achieve that goal, the more confidence you will gain and the better you will feel about tackling the larger, longer-range goals. Don't try to build Rome in a day; start slowly and let your confidence build. You can do this!

You can do it, unless you let yourself become derailed and lose sight of your goals. With all that you have become aware of to this point, how could you possibly not achieve your perfect life?

N

CHAPTER SEVEN

Falling Asleep At the Wheel

SELF-SABOTAGE

> *"You may be disappointed if you fail,
> but you are doomed if you don't try."*
> —*Beverly Sills*

There are any number of ways you can derail yourself. One of them is by thinking you can take shortcuts. It's called taking the easy way out, and it's often a bad idea. The only way to do a thing is to just commit to it and do it.

THE EASIEST WAY OUT REALLY ISN'T EASIER

Let's say you have designed a really wonderful life. You have dreamed of a huge home, several cars, a summer house, and all the trimmings. You see yourself as smarter than the average person, and you know you can figure out an easier way to have all of these lovely things other than doing the work it will take to achieve them. You have decided you don't want to plan or bother with the smaller goals in between now and then, and earning those things just takes too much time and effort. What avenue to owning those things is left to you? It usually will present itself to you as something illegal.

Pretend you decide you don't want to work for a living; that type of life is for chumps. You know a guy who drives a Porsche and lives in a huge house, and he got there by selling drugs. Okay, great. You have made a decision. You commit to that life. With the tools I have already given you, you should be able to see down this road and research the outcome, without actually having to physically go down the road. And in this case, not going down that road would certainly be an advantage.

Let's look at the situation closely. It is still going to take the same steps to achieve that goal as it would to achieve your dream in a legal and fulfilling manner. Although the steps are the same, the outcome could be radically different. You would have to make contact with a drug supplier, arrange for the pickups and deliveries, and cultivate the clientele. Sounds like goal setting and chunking to me. You would still have to physically do the work. In fact, there are a couple of extra steps you would have to take and extra goals you would have to achieve while doing something illegal rather than something legal and fulfilling. Those goals might be trying to ensure that you don't get caught or killed in some deal gone bad.

Those two steps would require careful and painstaking planning. There is one final decision you would want to make, assuming you have gotten this far in your goal. Who will live in that wonderful house and drive that beautiful Porsche while you are serving ten to twenty years in jail, or worse?

There is no easy way out. You are going to put just as much time and effort into doing illegal things as you are into doing legal things, and the potential for suffering is a whole lot higher. Do the research yourself. Just log on to the net and pull up some back issues of any major newspaper. It's not a matter of *if* you will lose everything you have worked for, but a matter of *when* you will lose it.

I would not recommend this route to your perfect life. I would discourage you in any way I can. It robs you of the joy of living a life you can be proud of and that your family can take pride in. It also robs the rest of us of the legitimate gift you have been given and are meant to share with us.

TRY NOT TO RUSH INTO LIFE

Rushing into life before you are ready is another way of derailing yourself. This can happen when you begin to realize how much life has to offer you, and how wonderful all those choices are. Life looks like a huge delicious meal and as you may be tempted to stuff it into your mouth all at one time. This isn't necessary and can be derailing. You can try to sample too much too soon. Be assured that everything will come to you in its own wonderful time and its own wonderful way. *Enjoy the time of life you are living now.* It is about as carefree and absent of stress as it will ever be. It's a mistake to try to become an adult too soon.

THERE WILL ALWAYS BE ROADBLOCKS AND PROBLEMS, BUT THAT'S OKAY

Being independent and making your own choices is terrific. Understand that along with those independent choices, come natural consequences that you will have to accept and deal with. You can have the perfect lifestyle and still have roadblocks and problems you need to solve. I am not promising that if you follow all the suggestions in this book you will never have any problems. There will be problems; it's a natural fact of life. I am saying that if you follow these suggestions, you will have much less trouble achieving a life that is best suited for you. When you do run into problems, you will be better prepared to overcome them if you chunk them down and solve them one step at a time.

Right now your problems and roadblocks are relatively simple and can be handled easily. Later in life you might encounter some really tough ones that will take a while to work through. Why borrow trouble now? Trying to grow up too soon can put you directly in line for financial or legal problems that you cannot work out yourself.

THE BIG THREE

The big three are drugs, drinking, and sex. You are all smart enough and aware enough of the dangers of drinking and drugs. That's pretty clear-cut. You have all heard the stories and you're aware of the consequences. They can take physical, emotional, legal, and financial tolls on you and your family that don't need to happen. It is your choice to invite those troubles into your life. You can avoid them altogether. Make the smart choice.

Sex is pretty clear-cut when you just look at the outcome by itself. However, it's not so clear-cut when you are emotionally involved and fall in love. When you meet someone you are attracted to and get along well, with you can become emotionally attached. You may even fall in love.

I have always hated the term "puppy love." I think it is condescending. For the time of your life you are living now, and the way you have experienced love up until this point, I think that if you proclaim love for someone else, it is as valid and real for you as it can be. Fortunately or unfortunately, depending on your perspective, your body's biological imperatives also begin to kick in during this time. Your body may be telling you that it is physically ready to handle sexual intimacy whether you are emotionally or financially ready for what the outcome of intimacy might be.

Now might be a good time to understand that young men and young women are emotionally different. They may not all be having sex for the same reasons. Love may not even enter the equation on one side or the other. I am not going to launch into a long discussion on sex or the moral aspects of it. I am only going to make you aware of the fact that love, followed by sex or plain sex alone, carries with it responsibilities. I am not going to list those—if you don't know what they are, don't engage in sex.

Before you do anything that cannot be undone, ask someone you love and trust who has the life experience to guide you in these matters. Ask a parent, your pastor or priest, a counselor—anyone but your peers. Your friends knowledge of the problems you might encounter probably doesn't extend much farther than your own knowledge does.

Misinformation is worse than no information at all. Find out what the ramifications of your actions might be. Becoming pregnant, having to marry the girl you got pregnant, or suffering from some sexually transmitted disease for the rest of your life can seriously put up major roadblocks to living your perfect life.

> *"Ninety percent of all those who fail were not actually defeated. They simply quit."*
> —*Paul J. Meyer*

One of the best billboards I have ever seen, and my personal favorite, said, *"Raising a baby costs $795 a month. How much is your allowance"?* Really think about growing up too soon. Take your time.

PROCRASTINATION

The next way you can derail yourself is by procrastinating. You can ignore everything I have said about when to start planning and setting goals for your perfect life and convince yourself there will always be time enough to achieve those goals—until you run out of time. You can ignore your education and put off your decisions until you find yourself on your own with no real life plan. You will find it much harder to support yourself and go back to pick up the skills you need to succeed. It is much easier to simply take advantage of the education when it is offered to you. Remember that public school is free, and you are being handed the skills you will need with no strings attached. Take advantage of that opportunity to its fullest.

THE LAZINESS FACTOR

There are times in your life that you can get into a rut. If you're in a rut, you may experience the feeling of not being able to get out of your own way. You may find you have no motivation. A lazy rut is one of these "hard-to-snap-out-of" ruts.

Standing alone, I don't think lazy is a terrible state. I believe there is a place for being lazy in our lives. We live in a world of yin and yang—opposites. For every night, we have a day, for every winter, we have a summer. Each serves its own specific purpose. It would then stand to reason that lazy, the opposite of hard-working, has a place in your world also.

There is nothing finer after a week of brisk activity than to have one day of quiet—nothing on your schedule, nothing pressing you into action. In fact, I believe that lazy can rejuvenate and refresh you. Having said all that, I do believe you can have too much lazy.

Because we live in a world of opposites, if we allow ourselves to become too indulgent in any one thing, we become out of balance, and we suffer because of that imbalance. Just as working too hard, for too long, can deplete you, too much laziness can ruin you in much the same way.

Laziness can perpetuate itself. By that I mean, the more time you spend doing nothing, the less you will feel like doing anything. If you have an unexpected snow day off from school and you spend it playing video games, no harm done. But if you spend so much of your free time glued to the television screen that your eyeballs are square, you are out of balance. Your body needs movement and exercise. Your mind needs new and different stimulation, and your spirit needs inspiration and challenge.

Laziness can mentally depress you. Before long, you will have trouble thinking of anything that would make you happy or anything you would rather do besides being lazy.

If you are in a lazy rut, there are several ways you can get yourself out of it. Call a friend and make some plans that don't involve just sitting around staring at each other. Play some hoops, go shopping, or swim. Even seeing a movie can stimulate your mind.

The cure for laziness is simply movement. Just begin to move, no matter what the movement. You will begin to find your body responding to activity and asking for more of the same. It doesn't take a rocket scientist to figure out that the cure for non-movement is movement.

If you find yourself lazy on the job, you don't have the right job. Your career should not leave you feeling drained or unable to move forward with the challenges it presents you. Perhaps you need to map out a new life design. Work should feel easy and fulfilling to you, while at the same time be challenging and exciting.

You may have to force yourself to try new and different things the first several times you are leaving your lazy rut, but if you are committed to breaking the lazy habit, be like Nike and "Just Do It." JUST MOVE! The hardest move will be off the couch.

DON'T LIMIT YOURSELF

Limiting yourself is another surefire way to derail your dreams. If you would love to go to medical school but have talked yourself into how hard it will be and how many hours it will take to get your M.D., then you have limited yourself. If you think you don't deserve a perfect life or you're not smart enough or not good-looking enough or not (fill in the blank) enough to achieve living your dream, then you have limited yourself. If your advisor on college admissions tells you that Duke is a really hard university to get into, and although you have the grades, you shouldn't even try, you have let that person limit you. If one of your classmates calls you stupid because you got an F in science, and you believe him and don't even try to raise that grade, he has limited you. Don't place limits on yourself or allow anyone else to place limits on you. You may not always excel at everything you try, but you may amaze yourself at the things you can accomplish and do well if you give it your best shot.

I will guarantee you that at this moment you are more than you even imagine yourself to be. You haven't even begun to tap into your potential, and if you allow yourself or someone else to limit your trying, you never will tap that potential. We are more willing to believe the negative things about ourselves than we are willing to believe the positive things. Be positive about and compassionate with yourself. Give yourself a break and allow for the possibility that you are more than you realize. *If you fail to try, you try to fail*. If you fail to master a skill you didn't have before, you have lost nothing in the trying of it. But if you don't try to master it, you will always live wondering, *What if I had tried?*

At the end of your life, "what if" should not enter your mind. Wouldn't it be better at eighty years of age, when you are rocking on your front porch, to say, "I tried some things and they didn't work out. I tried many others that I mastered. I have lived the life I wanted to live, and I have no regrets." No limiting should be a life rule you give yourself; it is a gift.

LEVELING AND HOSING

Throughout your life you will have the occasional unfortunate experience to run into people who have already limited themselves to the point they have become chronically insecure. These people usually become bullies. They are specialists at the arts of leveling and hosing.

Leveling is a way of pulling everyone down to the bullies level. They are so sure they are nothing themselves and are so envious of those who would try to succeed, they spend their time trying to pull other people down. If you let them, they will suck every bit of enthusiasm and drive you have for your dreams right out of you by trying to make you what they perceive as their size. An example of leveling is if you were excited by the prospect of sending an application to a college you really would like to attend and someone said to you, "You will never make it. It's a waste of time. I am not applying and you shouldn't bother either."

Hosing is only slightly different. It is the act of throwing cold water on any idea you might have. It's discouragement in the finest sense of the word. If you said, "Let's lay outside and get a tan today" and your friend said, "You're crazy, it's too hot," you have been hosed.

Notice that limiting, leveling, and hosing are all similar. There is only a fine distinction among all three. The intended outcome is the same for all three. They are all techniques aimed at keeping you from succeeding. You don't have to be able to define each one. Learn to identify this kind of behavior when you hear it, and don't allow it to affect your choices.

"If you fear making anyone mad, then you ultimately probe for the lowest common denominator of human achievement."
—Jimmy Carter

If you allow leveling or hosing to stop your drive, then you are limiting yourself. People who are negative and discouraging about your efforts or ideas cannot live your regrets if you do not follow through with your dreams. Think for yourself. Don't listen to these kinds of unconstructive comments. Instead, believe in yourself. Other people won't be living your life, and you are the expert in this area. There will be few obstacles you cannot overcome and few roadblocks you cannot work around if you look at your problems from different perspectives and choose a solution that will work toward your goals. The largest obstacle you will need to overcome is yourself and what you believe you are capable of. Believing anyone else's negative ideas about what you are capable of will only serve to make it twice as hard for you to achieve your dreams. You are already battling the subconscious core beliefs you have about yourself every day.

RESPOND, RATHER THAN REACT

Reacting to a situation rather than responding to a situation can also derail you. A reaction happens quickly and without thought. When a balloon suddenly pops behind your back and you jump, that's a reaction. If a puppy runs into the street in front of your car and you slam on the brakes, that's a reaction also. A reaction is outside of your conscious control.

Many people allow themselves to *react* to situations in their daily lives. If another person makes them angry or hurts their feelings, their immediate impulse is to react to the emotion. They can react in negative ways and cause more damage than good. Reacting also cuts off any possibility of finding a good solution to the situation at hand.

Responding is acting with thought and intent. You are conscious and deciding on the response you will choose to a situation. It allows for the possibility of solving the situation in the best way imaginable.

If a bee lands on your leg and you simply *react*, you may slap at the bee and end up getting stung. You didn't think about what you were doing—you simply went ahead and did it. If you *respond* to the bee on your leg, you may be calmer and may be able to simply brush the bee away to avoid getting stung. It is the same when dealing with other people.

If you run into someone in a crowed hallway and the other person calls you a clumsy idiot, you may react and hit the person or call the person a name back. This cuts off the possibility of ever getting to know that person, or worse, it may get you both suspended from school. In the same case, if you ran into someone and the person called you a clumsy idiot, and you replied that you were sorry, you weren't paying attention, you have opened the door to a peaceful solution and the possibility of having a friendship evolve.

You need not react. You can *respond* to any situation you run into. It is within your power and totally a matter of choice. The end result of a well-thought-out response will always be superior to an impulse reaction. The possibilities of derailing yourself by acting out of impulse far outweigh the possibility of derailing by a well-thought-out response. In fact, responding will keep you from derailing.

DON'T SET UNREALISTIC GOALS

You can also derail and sabotage yourself by setting unrealistic goals. Some of the goals you will set for yourself will not be solely within your control, and because they are dependent on the actions of other people, they may be unachievable. Others may not live up to their end of the bargain and your overall goal will not be met. While it is reasonable and realistic to expect that these people will be accountable for their part in the achievement of the goal, it is unrealistic of you to believe that nothing can go wrong. You may need to revise your plans and work around the roadblock the other person created. The best goals are those you control completely. Having said that, there will be plenty of goals in your life that will depend largely on someone else's action.

Another unrealistic expectation you can create for yourself is mistaking a dream for a goal. A dream is a dream until you put action behind it. Goals are not wishes; they are a collection of doable steps and plans that add up to a certain desired result. If you are five-feet, seven inches tall and you set your goal to be six-feet, three inches tall by the end of next week, chances are good you will not meet that goal. There are no doable steps you can take or control you can exert that will allow you to override your genetic code. Goals do not depend on luck. You must focus and do the work required to see them through. If you set a goal of winning the lottery, odds are against you in reaching this goal, too.

Everything you want in life is a goal that may be cleverly disguised in different clothing. Getting a new car begins with a goal. A deadline you must meet is a goal dressed in deadline's clothes. If your boss gives you a sales quota you must meet at the end of the month, the sales quota is just another name for a goal. Learn to see the language that disguises a goal. Practice goal setting now and learn how to achieve goals without panic or a sense of helplessness. This will only serve to move you to the front of the competition once you are out there on your own. Don't allow yourself to become derailed, and don't commit self-sabotage.

N

CHAPTER EIGHT

Flat Tires and Engine Trouble

MISTAKES, FAILURES, AND SUBCONSCIOUS CORE BELIEFS

*"It's not how many times you fall down,
it's how many times you get back up."*
—Anonymous

Subconscious core beliefs, mistakes, and failures are also other ways you can derail yourself, but I felt the discussion of these three topics was so important they needed a chapter of their own.

YOUR SUBCONSCIOUS

The subconscious mind is a complex and complicated system that occupies space somewhere in your brain. Explaining how it works could be a book of its own and, in fact, I don't think anyone knows exactly how the subconscious works in its entirety. You may get different theories depending on whose perspective you view it from. A psychiatrist may have a completely different theory than a dream analyst. For our purposes, I will just speak as generally and simply about how it works pertaining to subconscious core beliefs.

Your subconscious mind appears to you as an area of the brain that does not function every day. It seems to just lie around and eventually shows itself in the form of weird dreams or slips of the tongue. Actually the subconscious is a busy place. It's in action all the time; you are just not aware of its presence. One of its functions is to store information that you believe are your core truths. You don't have to remind yourself every day that you are either male or female because that fact is warehoused in the subconscious-core-belief area. It is so totally engrained in you, you never have to refer to the question of your sex.

The subconscious stores an enormous amount of facts and thoughts. It is necessary to move these facts and thoughts out of your conscious mind so that you can focus and concentrate on the thought you're having this minute. It keeps you from thinking every thought you have ever had all at the same time. You may describe one of its functions as a filtering process.

However, it places no filter on the *quality* of the ideas it stores; it makes no judgment. This means that it does not filter out the negative thoughts or ideas and only saves positive thoughts and ideas. The conscious mind makes the determination of judgment as you're having the thought and just passes it along to the subconscious for storage.

Whenever you need the material stored there, the subconscious acts like a computer. It pulls up the data you have logged in and hands it to you. This material does not come up as if it were on a real computer screen; it does not come up all at once and in great detail for you to sort through. It may come to you as a feeling, an idea, or an actual thought. In fact, if your conscious mind has judged an incident or information as being so stressful or traumatic to you, the subconscious may bury the information so deeply that you can't access it freely. This is what you are facing when you deal with subconscious core beliefs about your ability to achieve and excel.

You have many other subconscious core beliefs that are positive beliefs or beliefs that are not related to the way you feel about yourself in these success areas or the area of your self-esteem. I am just isolating this area of esteem beliefs to help you deal with the negative beliefs when they come up.

LET'S TALK ABOUT MISTAKES

We all make mistakes—lots of them. We all make mistakes privately, and we all make mistakes in the presence of other people. It's the way you tend to look at a mistake, or the perspective you assign to a mistake, that makes it a negative thing in your mind.

A mistake should be viewed as a miss take. Think of it in terms of making a movie. Movies are filmed scene by scene or step by step. Each time a director films a scene it is called a take. If take-one didn't work the way you wanted it to, then maybe take-two will, or perhaps it will be take-ten before it's perfect.

If you plan to do something, you go about the plan with a certain method in mind—an idea or way you will try to achieve the goal. If the method you chose does not work the first time, it's a miss take. You now know you tried it a certain way, it didn't work, and you can try again using another method. You don't repeat the first method, because you learned that it didn't work the first time, and there is no reason to expect that if you repeat the same method it will end with a different result, other than not working again.

> *"Anyone who has never made a mistake has never tried anything new."*
> *—Albert Einstein*

Mistakes should not be looked at with a negative connotation attached to them. It is a learning process in which you discover the best method by which to do something. There is no shame or blame in learning. I wonder how many tries it took Thomas Edison before he got the light bulb right? If Mr. Edison had quit trying after making the first mistake, we would all still be using candles.

AND NOW, ABOUT FAILURE

Failure is a mistake on a larger scale. Failures generally express the process of having a whole plan fall apart. One mistake in a project could lead to the project's failure. If you have failure of a whole project or even fail a school subject the first semester, it means that you made a mistake somewhere along the line and used a method that didn't work, which in the end caused the long-term goal to fail. You then need to go back, find out where your miss take occurred, and revise the methods you are using to allow the long-term plan to succeed.

> *"I haven't failed,*
> *I've found ten thousand*
> *ways that don't work."*
> *—Unknown*

Like the word "mistake," the word "failure" carries a negative connotation. It is a negative perspective on what is really happening. In fact, I believe that mistakes and failures are good. It means that you have at least tried something, and even though it didn't go the way you wanted it to, you learned what didn't work. If you know what doesn't work, you never have to do that again. So mistakes and failures don't hold you back as much as they move you forward. If you have to say you failed at something, look at it as failing forward. There is movement in the phrase "failing forward", but simply saying that I tried and failed can put an end to the learning process altogether.

You are making a mistake if you fail and *don't* try again. You need to try again so that you can fail forward and make more mistakes that will eventually allow you to reach your goal.

Mistakes and failures are not accidents. Accidents are just what the word sounds like—accidents. Knocking your glass of milk over at the table is an accident. You didn't make a goal of spilling your milk when you got to the table. You simply hit it with your arm and knocked it over. The spilled milk was an accident, not a mistake.

WHEN YOU VIEW MISTAKES, FAILURES, AND ACCIDENTS NEGATIVELY

I have taken the time to explain and define what mistakes, failures, and accidents really are and have enlightened you about the positive perspectives you should view them with to illustrate what viewing them with a *negative* perspective will do to your overall confidence and self-esteem. Viewing them with negative perspectives is also the birthplace of negative subconscious core beliefs.

When you make a mistake or experience a failure by yourself, you usually say something like, "Well, that was stupid." The conscious mind grabs that experience, judges it as stupid because you told it to call it stupid and sends it to the subconscious for storage.

The same thing happens when you make mistakes or experience a failure in front of someone else, only to a greater degree. No one likes to look clumsy or incapable by himself or herself, let alone in a group. If you make a mistake in front of someone, that person may say, "Boy, you are stupid." Again, the conscious mind grabs the experience, judges it as wrong because your friend told it to, and sends it to the subconscious for storage.

Now you have the idea or notion that you just might be stupid at worst, or just not smart enough at best, stored away in your brain's deepest memory bank. The impact of that message on you will be directly proportional to the embarrassment you felt when the incident occurred. If you were hugely embarrassed, the impact will be huge. If you continue to refer to yourself as stupid or accept anyone else's opinion about your intelligence, you are constantly reinforcing the idea that you are stupid, and you have given birth to a subconscious core belief about yourself.

From that moment on, whenever you try anything, that little subconscious core belief will pop up in your mind. It is not limited to attacks on your intelligence. A subconscious core belief will form around any negative idea you were given or have about yourself. After that, whenever you don't do something well or make a mistake in the same area as the original one, it will only serve to compound and reinforce the original subconscious core belief.

Subconscious core beliefs then gain so much power that they can actually stop you from trying anything new or succeeding at anything you try. Anytime you start a project or plan a goal, a subconscious core belief will be there to remind you that you are not good enough, strong enough, smart enough, pretty enough, or just plain not enough to succeed at what you're doing, and that you should not even try.

Even when you desperately want something, your subconscious core beliefs will be screaming to you, and you will listen. You will listen and believe your subconscious core beliefs because you listened before and either named the action stupid yourself or allowed someone else to do it for you.

Unfortunately, subconscious core beliefs are ready to develop when your brain begins to function and you begin to understand language. They get their start when you are too young to know how to recognize them for what they are and can consciously block them before they gain a foothold in your mind. They take hold the minute someone calls you stupid the first time you spill your milk. The little boy with the bad haircut, no front teeth, and a runny nose who tells you that you are ugly on the playground plants the first seed of your "I am not pretty enough" subconscious core belief.

Here is the really tough part of having subconscious core beliefs. They never go away. You cannot cure them. You cannot download, delete, expunge, or wish them away. No amount of self-talk or motivation will let you escape them. Once they are in the subconscious storage unit, they are there forever. It's an absolute fact, and there is no way around it.

HOW TO SHORT-CIRCUIT YOUR NEGATIVE SUBCONSCIOUS CORE BELIEFS

The good news is you can short-circuit those negative thoughts. You can outsmart them and achieve anything and you can do it in a grand fashion *if* you learn to recognize them when they pop up. You can derail them before they take hold of your actions. Subconscious core beliefs are sneaky devils.

If you hear "I can't do it" come out of your mouth, your subconscious core belief is screaming at you. In an instant it has reminded you of your last experience in this vein of endeavor and has convinced you that your current goal will end up the in the same fashion. "I can't" should be a clue for you to question yourself as to *why* you feel you can't do it. If there is no physical reason, and no reason other than the *feeling* that you can't do it, it's time to find out what subconscious core belief is trying to stop you.

You need to then ask yourself the question, "Why can't I do it?" You will get an answer. It will sound like this—you are not smart enough, pretty enough, strong enough, thin enough, good enough, athletic enough, articulate enough, outgoing enough or any combination ending with the words "not enough," to accomplish this goal.

Once you have isolated the lack in yourself that your subconscious core belief is trying to get you to believe, you can then derail it. You can think back and access the time this experience first happened to you and realize that the experience belongs to your history. You are no longer that person; you have grown and matured and learned much more than the person who first experienced that incident. Even if the original incident happened yesterday, you are not the same person you were yesterday; you're wiser and a day older.

Now here is the most important step—*you can choose to not believe your subconscious core belief.* You can say that you are smart enough, or whatever enough, and go ahead with your goal. It is at this point, when you have refused to believe your subconscious core belief, that you have beaten it. You can turn your back on the negative thought and move on to accomplishing whatever it is you want to accomplish. You may have to turn your back on the same subconscious core belief every time you set another goal. The more you recognize these thoughts and refuse to believe them, the easier it will be the next time, and the time after that, until you turn the screaming of your subconscious core beliefs into mere whispers.

MISTAKES AND FAILURES AS LEARNING TOOLS

Here is the really good news. You don't need to compound and grow the existing subconscious core beliefs you already own to more than what they are now, and you don't need to make any new ones, *if* you learn to recognize the statements or negative thoughts that allow them to be born in the first place.

Whenever you make a mistake or have a failure, do not refer to it as a negative experience and call yourself names or blame yourself. Get it, right now—

mistakes and failures are learning tools. There is no need to downgrade or belittle yourself for them. Nor are you to let anyone else do it for you. If you do make a mistake and someone calls you stupid, stop right then and say to yourself, "No, I am *not* stupid. I am learning and I am glad for the experience." Contradictory statements like that one will stop you from compounding any existing subconscious core beliefs or inventing new ones.

Subconscious core beliefs exist in all of us. There is no way you can live a normal life and not have given birth to several. They need not run your life. Learn to recognize that negative voice that seeks to prevent you from trying something. Question it, and when the negative belief rears its ugly head, turn your back on it.

If you allow it to run your life, it will stop you from trying new things, experiencing your life fully, and succeeding in living your perfect life. Just remember—subconscious core beliefs lie to you about what you are capable of. See the lie for what it is and cut the negativity off at the pass.

> *"If you stop trying now,*
> *then you'll never know*
> *what could have come*
> *of it in the future."*
> —A Nelson

N

Λ

CHAPTER NINE

Road Rage

COPING WITH YOUR DISAPPOINTMENT AND EMOTIONS

> *"Character may be manifested in the great moments,*
> *but it is made in the small ones."*
> *—Unknown*

This may be the first time you have been asked how you envision your perfect life, then again, your parents may be great natural coaches and you have had the opportunity to express your dreams before. Whatever the case, this book has been written to challenge you to think ahead to your future. It is necessary for you to do this; each choice you make today will affect your tomorrow. The seemingly small choices you never give much thought to can have a large and everlasting impact on the course your life will take.

Awareness of conscious choice is key in your life, and I have asked you to make some conscious choices here. In an effort to stimulate you, I have encouraged you to think outside the box and let your dreams about your future be large and fit exactly who you are as a person. I have asked you not to limit yourself or your ideas. I have wanted you to think in a specific manner about specific subjects and narrow down your answers to obtain clarity. While asking you to be concrete in your answers, I have asked you to be flexible also. This may seem like I am asking you to be absolutely sure, while at the same time I am telling you not to be. That's exactly what I am asking you. Flexibility is another key aspect of your life.

In the first chapter I talked about how to design a life or lifestyle you would be most happy living. It is your dream life. Chances are you have been dreaming about this before you ever opened this book. It may be so vivid, you can feel the wind blowing through your hair while you are driving your convertible Lexus SC 430 down the highway. You may even have it pinned down to knowing you want three children, two boys and a girl, and their names will be Jared, Jacob, and Jennifer. Great! Unless you don't get what you want and you have two girls and a boy, or all boys or no children at all. This chapter is about what to do if you don't get what you are dreaming of.

LIFE CHANGES AND THINGS HAPPEN

One thing you can be absolutely sure of in life is that it will change. Another thing you can count on is that there will be roadblocks and snags in your plans. Sometimes a plan won't work at all. Parts of your dream may be dependent upon the actions of another person. You may need a circumstance to fall into place at just the right time and nothing comes through for you. In other words, expect problems and disappointments. Expect things that do fall outside your control to go awry and alter your life design. Life is not perfect; it is not black and white. It's mostly gray and messy and juicy. It's also pretty wonderful; but things happen.

"If at first you don't succeed, you're running about average."
—M.H. Alderson

WHAT TO DO WHEN THINGS GO DOWN THE DRAIN

So what do you do when these "things" happen? What do you do when it looks like everything you wanted and planned for is going down the drain? Well, you can do one of three things. You can change your plans, you can stick to your plans and look for ways to work around the obstacles, or you can throw your hands in the air and scream, "I quit!"

QUITTING

Let's look at that quitting option first. So your original plans didn't work out as you had planned. There is no way you can get where you want to go from where you're standing now. You are tired of trying and you are discouraged. Nothing will turn out as you want it to anyway, so why bother? Go ahead and quit. Except you can't quit—not altogether anyway. You will go on living if you quit your plan, whether it's living your perfect life design or not. If you quit, you are giving yourself up to living a life that just happens by chance. It means that you are willing to accept much less than you hoped for yourself. It also means that everyone and everything around you will control your life and how it's lived. Doesn't sound very appealing, does it? Although quitting is an option, it has an undesirable and unacceptable result. So let's go on to the other two options and see if you can do better than this one.

> *"Here is a test to find whether your mission on Earth is finished. If you're still alive, it isn't."*
> —Richard Bach

QUITTING LIFE ALTOGETHER

One final word on quitting before moving on. Sometimes when people quit, they decide to quit life also. They become so depressed and discouraged that they just want to stop living altogether. They either do not *have* the tools or know how to *use* the tools to problem solve, and they become overwhelmed and quit.

Suicide is not an option. Suicide is an act. It is neither brave nor dramatic; it does not send a strong message. When people look back on suicides, they do not say, "Gosh, what a great solution!" It is cowardly and selfish and causes tremendous pain to those who love you.

Having said that, I will tell you that sometimes thoughts like that do run through your head, especially when times seem the toughest and it looks like your problems are unsolvable. I can't make my next point strong enough. If you are entertaining the idea of carrying out a suicidal thought, *GET HELP!* Things can look awfully dark at times, but there is no problem on earth that cannot be solved, and you must seek out people who will help you solve it. You are the only unique you we have on this planet. You carry with you a gift only you can give. Trust me when I tell you there is purpose to your life, even if you can't see it at the moment. Sometimes the moment of quitting comes just before the most profound success. Turn to those you trust, and if you don't have trust in your life, find a professional or call a hotline. But *GET HELP!*

CHOOSING ANOTHER OPTION

Instead of quitting and letting your dream go, let's look at changing your plan option. Let's say you wanted to go to medical school and just couldn't get in. You need to ask yourself what happened in your planning stages that produced this result.

Sometimes you overlook your red flags and push on even though the plan will obviously not work. Perhaps you were not realistic in your goals. Did you ignore the fact that your grades weren't good enough, or perhaps you test poorly? Did you apply to enough medical schools, or were you pinning your hopes on just one? Was it actually you? Perhaps if you called the medical school itself and asked why you didn't get in, it will enlighten you.

You need to investigate all the possibilities of what went wrong. You don't want to repeat the same method and have it fail again for an avoidable reason.

If you find you did everything you could to make your plan happen and it still didn't, then you need to simply make a new plan. Choose another option.

> "The bumps in the road just make the ride more fun."
> —Jorj Wager

I assure you, if you keep an open mind, you will find another profession that will serve you as well. You are not a one-dimensional being who has only one destiny. You are multidimensional, and you will find other destinies that will lead you to the same perfect life—if you keep your mind open. It is not the end of the world.

Sometimes, as hard as it is to believe, the best answer is no. You may not see the reason for a while, but eventually you will see that, even though you crashed and burned, out of the ashes came the best, most perfect solution you could have wished for. When one door shuts, another opens.

STICKING TO YOUR PLAN

Which brings me to the next and last option—sticking to your plan. If your plan didn't work and it looks like you may have to change your plan, don't do anything rash. Go back to find out *what* about the plan didn't work.

For example, if you didn't get into medical school and you retraced your steps and found out that, instead of you not having high enough grades, the school was already full, you can simply alter your plan. Go to another college for a year and reapply to as many medical schools as you can, and apply at the earliest date.

Perhaps your grades were a point or two shy of the entrance requirements. Go to that other college for a year. Pull your grades up to meet the requirements and apply for a transfer to the medical school. The point is, you won't know the reason why your plan failed to happen unless you *look* for the reason. If the reason turns out to be something that can be fixed or altered to allow the plan to continue, then you must be willing to do those things that will make that final goal happen. If you're going to stick to your plan, *find out what went wrong and correct it.*

COPING WITH DISAPPOINTMENT

Don't let disappointment stop you or get you so tightly in its grips that it leads to a huge depression. Don't let it cloud your vision. There are ways to cope with disappointment so that it won't take over your life.

Are you allowed to be disappointed? Absolutely! In fact, I plan for my disappointments. Personally, when I am disappointed that some plan of mine hasn't worked out, I give myself a day to wallow in it. I give myself twenty-four hours in which I can shut myself away from the world and really fell sorry for myself. I cry, and I go ahead and allow myself to lay blame on everything and everyone I can think of. I lie around the house all day and do nothing but eat chocolate. I acknowledge my disappointment. Heck, it was my plan and it didn't work out, so I allow myself to feel that and just throw on a great pout. Why pretend it's okay if it's not? After giving myself that day to wallow, the next day I get up, shower, stop blaming anything or anyone else, and take a hard look at why my plan didn't work.

The ideal thing for you to do before you run up against disappointments—and trust me, you will—is make a plan for how you will deal with them *before* you're faced with them. Call it your disappointment plan. You know better than anyone else how you will react to disappointments or obstacles. Figure out what actions will allow you to vent your disappointment in a healthy way. Rule out the ones that will be destructive to you (you may not break into your parents' liquor cabinet or throw yourself in front of a train) or hurt others (you may not use your little brother as a punching bag).

Set a time limit for your wallowing. I told you my time limit was a day. Any more than a day and I am afraid it would become a habit for me. The last thing you want to do is get in the habit of feeling sorry for yourself. So keep your time limit short. Setting a time limit also has another benefit. It provides you with your very own light at the end of the tunnel. You know that the end of your disappointment time is designated. You can wallow, free from the fear that you won't be able to get yourself out of it. When your wallowing time is up, it's up, and it's a signal for you to start solving your problems.

Have fun with your disappointment plan. Create a list of all the things that comfort you when you're feeling depressed or upset. My friend likes to lock herself in the bathroom and soak in a bubble bath until she looks like a prune. While she is soaking, she eats ice cream and cries. I like a touch of naughty in my wallowing, so I throw on the forbidden sweatpants, get out the Oreo cookies, and cry. Remember, it's only for one day, so a bit of rebellion won't hurt. Just don't take it too far.

If you like to go shopping when you're blue, now is the time to set a limit on your spending spree. If you wait until you're in the throes of disappointment, you may spend way too much and create bigger, different problems for yourself.

In the space on the next page, write out the plan you will use when you run up against a disappointment. Here are a couple of ideas. Build a fire in the fireplace and wrap up in your favorite blanket with a good book. Eat some naughty, fattening comfort foods that you save only for occasional treats. Jog, work out, get out your magazines, and draw over all the models so they look fat.

Guys—your methods of wallowing are different. Males tend to work out their disappointments in more physical ways. Call a buddy and shoot hoops all day. Play racquetball and pretend the ball is the object of your disappointment. Run a couple of miles or lift weights. Have fun with this. Be creative and make your plan now.

In the space below, write down your ideas for dealing with disappointment. Use some of the ideas on the previous page to help you.

_____

_____

_____

_____

_____

_____

_____

_____

_____

_____

_____

_____

_____

_____

_____

_____

_____

_____

_____

_____

_____

_____

_____

_____

_____

_____

_____

Good job. Now that you have a plan for coping with your disappointments, remember to use it when you encounter a disappointment, or even when you're a bit down.

MANAGING YOUR EMOTIONS

Understand that holding disappointment inside or pretending to yourself and to everyone else that it just isn't a big deal will make things worse. If you don't find a way to get rid of your disappointment in a *good* way, it will only fester underneath the surface and explode later on, probably at the moment when an explosion will cause the most damage.

You might do something on the spur of the moment that you will regret forever. Some things in life you cannot take back. Words hurt and are remembered. If you lash out at someone who has done nothing except make the mistake of being in the wrong place at the wrong time, you may forever damage a relationship or friendship.

Physically punishing yourself or someone else is out of the question. It is not an option here; it never will be. Learn to manage your feelings. You will not feel

> *"Holding on to anger is like grasping a hot coal with the intent of throwing it at someone else; you are the one who gets burned."*
> —Buddha

like making a plan to vent your disappointment when it happens. Therefore, it's good that you took the time to plan ahead. When it does happen, you can just get out your plan and slip into it. At the end of the time you have allotted for yourself, the worst part of your disappointment will be over. You can move on to the solution to the problem at hand with a clear head.

Managing your anger can be done in the same manner. Anger can happen at any time, and any situation or person can trigger those feelings of anger. Anger unleashed is an example of reacting to something rather than responding to it. Take a moment to source the problem and figure out how to correct it without lashing out.

> *"A man is measured by the size of things that anger him."*
> —Geof Greenleaf

If you can't source the problem, make a plan for venting your anger that includes no one else. If it's a person with whom you're angry, it's okay to tell that person you are angry and to please leave you alone for a while. Remove yourself from the person or situation immediately. Go for a walk to cool down. Find your punching bag or a pillow. Take a quick run or a sprint. Do anything that will immediately satisfy the urge to strike back. Trying to solve a problem while you are angry will not work and may ultimately make the matter much worse. Only after you have calmed down and thought the matter through will you be able to tackle the problem in an effective way.

While it is true that you cannot plan when emotions will happen, *you can plan what to do when you feel them come up*. The good emotions, like love or humor, have nice reactions and need not be planned for. However, the emotions that could cause you to make mistakes or have regrets should be planned for. Remember, one of your goals is to make your life as easy and pleasant as you possibly can. Trying to correct mistakes and live with regrets should be something you plan to eliminate.

Start thinking now about a plan that will be effective for dealing with your feelings when they come up. Use the space on the next page to sort out your thoughts.

In the space below, write down your ideas for dealing with feelings that may cause you to make mistakes or have regrets. Use some of the ideas on the previous page to help you.

_____

_____

_____

_____

_____

_____

_____

_____

_____

_____

_____

_____

_____

_____

_____

_____

_____

_____

_____

_____

_____

_____

_____

_____

_____

_____

_____

THE BREATH MOMENT

Now that you have your disappointment and anger plan made, putting it into action at the appropriate moment will be so much easier if you practice a technique I call the breath moment.

I have learned through the years that the easiest way to prevent myself from reacting to a situation, rather than responding to the situation, is to automatically give myself a moment to remember that I can choose which way I will respond. I would much rather respond in a good way than react and regret it. I am in control of this choice. I inhale one deep breath, and in the time it takes to inhale, I remind myself of control. That's usually all it takes— just a second to remember that I wish to respond. Whether I know how to respond at the moment, or I need to remove myself from the situation before I know how to respond, the key is giving myself the breath moment before I do anything.

Develop a breath moment for yourself. It gives you the time you need to stop before you do anything else and exercise your choice. It has saved me countless times from doing something for which I would have been sorry later.

N

CHAPTER TEN

Rules of the Road

BUILDING YOUR LIFE ON A STRONG FOUNDATION

> *"Try not to become a man of success,*
> *but rather try to become a man of Value."*
> *—Albert Einstein*

While you are busy setting your short-term and long-term goals, you will want to keep in mind, the principles by which you will live your life. Your goals and dreams, and the way in which you achieve them and live your life in general will, need to have standards attached to them.

NEGATIVELY IMPACTING ANOTHER PERSON'S LIFE

Your life in general should not negatively impact another's life. Notice I said *should not*. Sometimes this is unavoidable under certain circumstances. If you are a salesman, for example, and you and a coworker are competing for salesman of the month and you win, you have technically negatively impacted his or her goal. I am not saying that you should back down and just let the coworker win; I *am* saying that if you did it in a good way and with high standards, then it is an example of healthy competition. Wherever there is competition, there will be a winner and a loser. If the winner has won without cheating and in a good manner, this is not what I would call negative impact.

Impacting the world or those around you in a negative way is a more manipulated effort on your part. If the dream of owning a house by the water requires you to destroy several acres of natural wetlands, you should rethink the plan and come up with another. If you win recognition at work for a great idea, but you took the idea from a coworker, that's negative impact. I can argue these types of points all day, but I feel that you know what negative impact is or is not in the context with which I am writing it.

YOUR STANDARDS AND RULES

There are certain standards you can set for yourself that you should be thinking about now. These will aid and guide you throughout your life. There are a few that will become tools for you to use for your own protection and self-esteem. These standards are called foundation principles. They will become very much a part of who you are and how you will operate in life. You will define them for yourself, and you will be defined by them.

Chapter 1 briefly introduced you to foundation principles, protection rules, and conduct rules. Let me elaborate. .When you were too young to understand these principles, you were given a foundation by your parents, school and/or church. The easiest words for defining foundation principles are "rules to live by."

When you were young, these rules were imposed for your protection. *You may not play in the street* is an example of a protection rule. As you got a little older, your parents no longer had to repeat and reinforce this rule, because you were able to understand the wisdom of staying out of the traffic for yourself.

The more you grew, the more the rules changed. As you began to interact with others, your rules included how you conducted yourself in society. No biting, no hitting and no pulling of hair are examples of conduct rules. Unfortunately, some people still don't have this one down, but I am sure you get the drift of the example. The rules changed and matured as you did.

Your school also has a list of rules. They are meant to keep order and facilitate a quiet atmosphere in which everyone can learn. You may not understand the need for some of these rules. I never got the gum-chewing rule. I couldn't see what harm it would do if someone chewed gum. I came to understand through personal experience that the rule was made for two reasons.

Reason one I discovered when I sat in front of a woman at the movies who was chewing gum. She chewed with her mouth open, and she liked to pop her gum a lot. She sounded like a cow trying to pull its foot out of the mud, and because of the noise, I couldn't enjoy the movie at all. I could neither concentrate nor hear well. The second reason became clear when I happened to pass the janitor's office and saw him down on his knees scraping old hard gum off the bottom of the desks. I realized that the school was paying him by the hour to reverse the damage caused by someone's nasty habit.

Your church or spiritual center also has rules that it would like you to follow. They are more like a blueprint to use through your life. These, too, are rules for you as an individual to guide the way in which you function at home or in society.

There are always reasons behind rules. You may not think that those reasons are valid, but at some point, someone has done something that necessitated making a rule. Rules are also necessary. Imagine the chaos we would be in if anything and everything went. No red-light or stop-sign rule, no rule against burning when it was dry, stealing was okay—the possibilities boggle the mind.

I believe in the importance of rules, and the way in which they are best observed and followed is when you think them out for yourself, like I did with the gum chewing. When they become personal and important to you, you remember them. Remember back in the beginning chapter when I told you I believed that we do a good job of teaching our children to learn, but we don't really teach them how to think? Well, this is an example of that statement.

You have grown up with all these rules. Some you understand—they are obvious—and some you don't understand unless someone explains them to you. You have lived by the rules for the very young, rules for the medium young, and

> "Character is what you are in the dark."
> —Unknown

then rules for the mature young. These rules have changed in type and content, because while growing, you were maturing into accountability for your own actions. This happened in stages, and the rules changed for each stage. Add to the mix the social guidelines you got along the way to help you interact well with others, like *don't gossip* or *don't talk behind someone's back*. What you ended up with was this huge list of rules that were made for you and enforced all the way through your childhood.

You never had to think about rules; they were just there for you to follow, which isn't a bad thing. In fact, it's a very *good* thing. They kept you safe and ensured the order of your world. Now you are graduating from school and heading out into the world—a really big and awesome place. It has rules of its own to follow, but they are not nearly as closely enforced as the rules in school were.

Many of those school rules will not apply anymore. You can chew gum if you want, and you can run in the hallways if you need to. You will be confronted with new experiences and situations you have never had before, so how will you conduct yourself now? Now you need to have rules and guidelines that work for you in a different, more compelling way, and you may never have given a thought as to how to make them for yourself.

When my son was young, a friend of his wanted to borrow his car for the night. My son asked me about it. It seems that the friend didn't have a car because he didn't drive well and had wrecked his. This caused my son some concern, and he really didn't want the friend driving his car, but because they were buddies, he didn't know how to say no. I told my son to tell him it was a policy of his to never lend his car to anyone. He did, and the friend just asked somebody else. What I didn't explain to my son was that this was called a boundary and that you made these rules or policies for yourself.

In fact, I don't remember sitting down and explaining thoroughly any of the guidelines I gave my children in terms of naming them as the foundation principles. I can't remember saying, "This is a value or this is an ethic." I did, however, correct this later on, but not when they still lived in my home. My hope is that they did not encounter situations in the meantime for which they were not prepared.

Living your life without foundation principles that you have thought about and set for yourself is like going out to cut down a tree with a table knife. You are poorly equipped for the job.

You will still keep the biggies from childhood—*don't kill anyone, don't steal, don't lie,* etc. But now you have to add your own rules. You must think for yourself about what rules you want and which ones will serve you well. You must believe in your rules or they will not serve you. Your parents and your schools are not driving your bus anymore; *you* are driving your bus. So I am inviting you to think about the rules that you will be finally setting for yourself.

How do you want the world to perceive you as an adult? Do you want your coworkers, neighbors, and friends to see you as honest? Sincere? Insincere? Irresponsible? Jealous? How do you want your peers to describe you? How do you ensure that your actions will be constant and reliable? By having well-thought-out foundation principles that you have taken to heart and can live by—that you don't even need to think about to use.

I am going to give you a list of examples of what foundation principles could be, followed by a brief explanation, a couple of questions, or a statement I would like you to think about. These are some of the things that I feel are important and that are in my own foundation principles.

> *"You cannot be strong in the big important things if you are weak in the little things."*
> —Ralph S. Marsten, Jr.

They are "my" opinions. You do not have to agree. I am not saying you have to have all of these or just this many. These are things that are important to me, and they may or may not be my entire list. You are not wrong if you do not include the same things I have included. You are not wrong if you disagree with me. The only point of giving you my thoughts and opinions is to stimulate you to think for yourself.

SPIRITUALITY

This is a biggie for me. It's also the toughest one to discuss because it is the most personal. It need not be a biggie for you, but I find that I am grounded and comforted by it. Whatever your spiritual preference or religion, or not, make sure that you understand its dogma that and it works for you. If it doesn't work for you, find something that does, or not. It's your choice. This is a personal preference and a set of beliefs, and they need to be right for you.

If you are seeking something to believe in now, just let me say this word of caution. If you run across a group or religion that seeks to control your actions or the actions of another at the mere whim of its leader, then *RUN*. If you are so insecure about your own personal power that you seek to join a group or religion that will try to control or harm others, get yourself some professional help.

BOUNDARIES

Boundaries are set up for your protection as well as to set limits on your actions. Everyone needs boundaries. They define for others how you expect to be treated, and they keep you from imposing on anyone else. They work both ways, both limiting and protecting at the same time. If you don't want to be hit, don't ever allow anyone to hit you. If you don't have money to lend friends, or you don't want to have an awkward conversation when they don't pay you back, set a boundary against lending money.

When they ask to borrow money, you can be ready with your boundary answer, and then it will not be awkward. You can say it with a smile and move off the subject. Tell them, "My policy is never lending anyone money." Done. They will not come back and ask again, because you have set your boundaries. You can set any boundary for yourself that you want.

I would prefer you didn't smoke in my home. I don't lend out my clothes. Anything that serves you. You are not obligated to fit your friends into your monthly budget or allow someone to take the clothing you worked hard to buy. It's totally up to you. What boundaries will you make to protect yourself? Think about what you want and don't want in your life. If you have a set of boundaries in place when you need them, they will serve you well.

Now think about what boundaries you will place on yourself. How far will you allow yourself to go? One of my personal boundaries was made long ago after seeing one of my girlfriends get plastered in public. I remember thinking how totally unattractive she looked, falling all over everyone with vomit on her blouse. It was then that I made this boundary for myself—I refuse to humiliate myself by drinking to excess.

On the next two pages, make two lists—how you want others to treat you (your protection), and how you will treat yourself (your limits).

"You were born an original. Don't die a copy."
—John Mason

In the space below, write your ideas about how you want others to treat you. Use the guidelines from the previous prages for ideas.

_____

_____

_____

_____

_____

_____

_____

_____

_____

_____

_____

_____

_____

_____

_____

_____

_____

_____

_____

_____

_____

_____

_____

_____

_____

In the space below, write your ideas about how you want to treat yourself. Use the guidelines from the previous prages for ideas.

_____

_____

_____

_____

_____

_____

_____

_____

_____

_____

_____

_____

_____

_____

_____

_____

_____

_____

_____

_____

_____

_____

_____

_____

_____

_____

ETHICS

Ethics is about discerning and practicing what is right and what is wrong. It is about doing the right thing, even when no one else is looking. Is stealing only stealing when you get caught, or is it determined by the size of what you take? Do you help yourself to the grapes while you grocery shop? Ethics is also about respecting yourself enough to have the integrity to want to do the right thing. Most businesses have a code of ethics for working in the world that you will be expected to adhere to and use. Be sure to read this code of ethics and understand what it means. Make your own personal code of ethics to live by.

VALUES

Values are the things you practice that you find value in. You use manners—please and thank you—because they have value to you. They are tricky devils, because values are something you give others that you would like to have returned in a similar manner to yourself. Having someone say please and thank you to you means something in your life. What do you find valuable? Courtesies, punctuality, manners, honesty, truthfulness, stability, friendship, and humor are all values. Because you value them, you will most likely exhibit them in your behavior. Think about what you value most from your friends and what you would like to practice in return. Like I said, values can get tricky. Here is why.

You can unconsciously use values to manipulate others. They can become all about you and nothing about your self-worth or giving to other people. For example, if your friend has a really nice dress on today, and you value compliments enough to practice complimenting, you might say to her, "I love your dress." You are using complimenting to manipulate her into complimenting you back. The "I love your dress" statement says nothing about her; it merely states your opinion and is solely about you and your taste. Notice there is an *I* and not a *you* in the statement. A better way of complimenting her would be, "You look lovely in that dress." Notice that there was not a reference about you in that statement.

If you wish to guard against the idea that you could manipulate with values, just have no expectations that anyone will ever be polite or courteous back. Give what you value without having expectations of getting it back. Use your values because you think they are important and define what kind of person you are.

ACCOUNTABILITY

Accountability is simply the act of being able and willing to take responsibility for your actions. If I say I am going to meet the deadline on Friday, and I don't meet the deadline, I am accountable for the missed deadline. It was my action and no one else is to blame. Responsibility weighs heavily in this one for me, so I combined these two. I feel if I am accountable, then I have already accepted the responsibility for my actions. This wasn't always so. I had to think about this just like you will have to think about it.

I had two dogs through my high-school years that were falsely held accountable for me not handing in my homework. But claiming that the dog ate your homework will not work when you join the adult ranks. Accountability is the decision to take responsibility for and control of your life. Get straight with it and accept it. There is nothing worse than a whiner who blames everyone else for his or her problems.

> *"To decide to be at the level of choice is to take responsibility for your life and to be in control of your life."*
> *—Arbie M. Dale*

This also extends to contracts. If you have roommates and you sign the lease, the phone application, and the heating contract, you will be held accountable. If your phone bill ends up being $800 one month because Sally was calling her boyfriend long distance constantly, and Sally can't come up with the dough for her share, the phone company will not care. You cannot use the excuse that your roommate made those calls and not you. You signed a contract

> *"The best years of your life are the ones in which you decide your problems are your own. You do not blame them on your mother, the ecology or the President; you realize you control your own destiny."*
> —*Albert Ellis*

saying that you would be accountable for the bill, and it will, at the end of the day, either be your money that pays it or your credit that will suffer. Always understand completely before you sign anything that will make you accountable for it.

SELF-ESTEEM OR SELF-CARE

This one is personal to me also because of my own life experience. I feel it's worth mentioning, because after my experience, I noticed a lot of other people I saw on the street who must have been experiencing the same thing. I went through a divorce and was suffering from mild depression. My mother became ill and passed on while I was going through my own trauma. It only served to compound my issues.

It wasn't until a good deal of time had passed before I met someone whom I came to trust as a good mirror for me. One day he said, "You need a makeover", and even though it hurt my feelings a bit, I kept an open mind and decided to have a good look. When I did, I was horrified. What I saw was a woman whose self-esteem had been so neglected that her self-care had suffered. Looking back now, I see how it happened.

I was blue and didn't feel like going out much, and at that point I had no time limit on wallowing. I stayed in and comforted myself with food treats. Since I wasn't going out, I didn't need to dress up and I wore sweatpants a lot. (Let me give you a tip—never wear sweatpants for longer than a couple of hours. Never wear them day-to-day; they lie). I had also let my hair grow and the style did not suit me at all. I seldom put on makeup and I didn't read the newspaper, so I couldn't have held a current interesting conversation if my life had depended on it. There was nothing left to do but turn myself around.

I embarked on a total self-care program. I changed my diet, joined a gym, hired a trainer, and began to wear makeup again. I had my hair cut and styled and bought new clothes that flattered me as I lost each dress size. I began to watch the news again and went back to school for some additional education. I thank my friend, who has now become my husband, everyday for loving me enough to tell me the truth. It makes me cringe every time I think I presented myself to the world in that way.

I don't care how much you argue with me that people should not judge others by their appearance. I won't believe you. Your appearance and how you treat yourself will always be a measure of how you will treat others and how you feel about any work you undertake. If you are sloppy and outdated, it will come across to others that your work will be sloppy and outdated. What the world will know about you at first glance will be determined by what kind of self-care you practice. Be as kind to yourself as you can be; enjoy who you are. If you enjoy massages and they make you feel great, don't look at them as a luxury; look at them as a necessary part of your self-care.

Make time for your hobbies and your relaxation. They are a crucial part of your life and keep you relaxed and refreshed. You will be able to do your job in a much better fashion. Take care with your clothing and your hair. Make sure your fingernails are clean. When meeting someone, your first impression will stick.

I understand that there are professions in which you would not wear your best clothes. Construction workers or auto mechanics cannot wear their good clothes to work. However, when you are out on Friday night, take care that you do not look like you just crawled out from underneath a car.

I see people on the street every day who do not have this foundation principle. Their hair is not clean and they look like they ran through their closet, and whatever fell on them, they wore. What a huge disservice this is to you. Before my own experience, I would have judged them as low class; now I have much more compassion. They are moving through their lives in an unconscious and unaware state, just as I had. I wish someone would tell them how important it is to have self-esteem and self-care in their foundation. Have this principle so engrained in you that you need not think about it. How you present yourself speaks volumes about who you are. It is the first definition that others will get before they even speak to you.

This is an example of what foundation principles are. They are things you believe in that define you and that are so engrained in your everyday life you practice them without having to think about them. They become positive subconscious core beliefs. I am asking you to think about these examples and see where you stand with them. On the next page, make a list of foundation principles for yourself. It will change and grow as you experience new things. You may end up with a long list or a short one. It's your list and, as always, it's your personal choice. The only requirements you must for having foundation principles are that you believe in them, and that they serve you every day. The more you practice these principles, the less you will have to consciously call them to mind. Pretty soon, they will just be who you are and what the world sees when they look at you.

In the space below, write your ideas about your foundation principles. Use the guidelines on the previous pages to help you get your thoughts organized.

_____
_____
_____
_____
_____
_____
_____
_____
_____
_____
_____
_____
_____
_____
_____
_____
_____
_____
_____
_____
_____
_____
_____
_____
_____
_____
_____
_____

N

Λ

CHAPTER ELEVEN

It's Not About the Destination, It's All About the Journey

THE RIPPLE EFFECT

"What really distinguishes this generation in all countries from earlier generations, is its determination to act, its joy in action, the assurance of being able to change things by one's own efforts."
—Hannah Arendt

In the past chapters you made choices about the type of life you dream of living and made lists that inventory what you know about yourself at this moment. I invited you to think about your principles—the rules you will set for yourself while pursuing your perfect life. It was all fun and pretty simple to do. All it required on your part was thinking and making conscious choices for yourself. You looked at the emerging threads or clues as to who you really are and what you really believe, in a simple and fun way. You had the opportunity to view how complete you are becoming through fun and simple exercises. Notice I keep repeating the words "simple" and "fun."

> *"I have heard it said that the first ingredient of success—the earliest spark in the dreaming youth—is this; dream a great dream.*
> *—John A. Appleman*

This is not brain surgery, folks. This is simple and fun. What it requires from you is just being aware that you are making choices and that you are conscious of what those choices are. I am asking you to dream about your future and see your highest vision of what you want to become in that future. It becomes a simple matter of choosing to allow the dream to become a goal for you.

That long-range goal can then be chunked down into smaller short-range goals that will lead you backward from the achievement of that long-range perfect life goal to where you stand today. Today is your starting point. Having chunked your perfect life down into a series of steps and smaller goals, you will see in no uncertain terms that *the choices you are making today have a tremendous impact on how you will be able to live your life tomorrow.*

There is a simple and clear-cut path to achieving this goal, to living your dream. Your life does not have to rely on luck or chance or the whims of other people. You are in control here. You are the expert on your life, and the method you are using to stay in control of your life is simple. The key lies in the awareness of well-thought-out, conscious choice to support the goal from this day forward. It is yours for the taking. You can achieve anything and everything you want by simply allowing yourself to believe in your potential.

I don't think you have a clue as to how extraordinary and capable you are. I wrote this book because there is a good chance you could vastly underestimate yourself and not live the limitless potential I know you have. I would really like you to invest in your potential and live a life of fulfillment and abundance. The best way I know how to do this is to encourage you to dream.

Your dream is the voice of your potential urging you on to accomplishment. Your dream is your potential teasing you with the possibilities of your life. I want you to be aware of your dreams. I want you to see those dreams, not as wanderings of your mind, but with awareness that what you dream is truly possible.

Get in touch with what you really want to do with your life. Let your thoughts be without limits, and let your goals be large.

Having a life of abundance filled with all the material luxuries you dream about is a wonderful and pleasant outcome to achieving your perfect life. It is not the only benefit, nor is it the best benefit you will receive. As I said before, money cannot buy you happiness, but it can make you comfortable while you're miserable. Money is just one currency in your

> *"You are where you are in life because of what you think is possible for yourself."*
> —*Oprah Winfrey*

life. It is, however, an important currency. You may think that having all the designer clothes you want, or driving a certain sports car and living in a big home, would be pretty hard currencies to beat, but let me assure you, there is much more to living an extraordinary life than this.

Money is a currency that we have created to reward ourselves for our efforts. When you work at your career or profession and serve society, then it rewards you with money. The better you are at your career or profession, the more rewards you receive. It is important to be financially independent and be able to care for yourself and your family. It is important to make enough of this monetary reward for you to feel comfortable in your daily life. If you never have enough money for the essentials in life like food, clothing, and shelter, then you will spend all of your time trying to provide yourself with those things. Your life will revolve around your basic survival.

This book is not just about making money and about what material things you can own with money. Nor is it about making wealth wrong. The emphasis here is not solely about money, but about everything that comes along with a perfect, well-lived life. Whatever judgment you place on money and wealth is your judgment and your choice. I am simply telling you what is. This is how we have created our society to work. To allow you to think that money is everything in life, or the reverse, that money should not be a consideration in your life, would be misleading on my part.

A dream is not a reality. Dreams are lovely ideas that must be made into goals before they can be achieved. You may dream that money is not an important factor in a wonderful life; however, it is just a dream. We must all live and deal with the reality of *what is* in life, and realistically, money plays an important role in the world we have created for ourselves.

Money is a tool we invented to obtain the things we need in life to survive and to buy the things we desire above survival. Which side you take on its importance is up to you, but it is a measure of success in the eyes of society. However you feel about this, let's set aside the money issue for a moment and take a look at what other currencies go into a life well lived.

If you have a life map and know yourself well, you may then set your goals and use your gifts and talents to achieve any amount of financial independence you wish. While using your brilliance and potential to achieve independence, you will be opening yourself to receive the other extraordinary currencies that come with a perfect life.

> *"Life is a great big canvas; throw all the paint on it you can."*
> —Danny Kaye

One of the ingredients to having a fulfilled life is using your talents and skills to their fullest potential. I believe that each of you is born with a gift or genius. That gift is as individual to you as your fingerprints. Each of you can do something better than anyone else in the world. That gift is meant to be expressed and shared with the world.

Discovering your gift is what this book is all about. You will know when you have discovered your gift because there will be passion behind it. The very idea of your gift will excite you. You will want to express your gift, and it will become your life's work.

Allow your life's work to have passion. When you work with passion, something extraordinary happens in your life. You greet each day with joy and enthusiasm; excited by the possibilities and challenges you will meet. That joy and enthusiasm will encourage you to be limitless in what you will achieve with your work. By its very definition, limitless means without end. There will be no end to what you can achieve!

Passion also seeks its own level of excellence. If you work with passion, you will constantly raise your own bar of standards for your personal best. Your gift, and the genius in that gift, will come shining through for the entire world to see. Your work will become a currency for you. You will move mountains to see that the goals you have set for yourself in your profession are achieved. The currency of recognition from others for excellence in your profession will be met. When passion is behind your work, you will excel, and abundance will follow that excellence.

I have been talking about you as an individual and your individual achievements. So far you have excavated your gifts and talents and have mapped a life that is perfectly suited to you around those talents. You will become financially independent because you have found your passion for your life's work. You have set standards, which will become your foundation principles and you have learned how to overcome disappointments and roadblocks. I haven't even begun to touch on what that means in relationship to the other people in your life. How can just these steps affect the quality of the relationships in your life? It is called the ripple effect.

When you drop a big stone in a pond, the initial drop causes a big splash. Out from that big splash come ripples that travel to the banks of the pond. The circles get increasingly wider and wider as the ripples move out, taking in more and more of the pond until the ripples reach the shoreline. Imagine that you are this big stone and the pond is the rest of the world. You are becoming a rock-solid, complete force that is being dropped into the world; along with the gifts and tools you have just developed. The splash that you make in the pond of the world and the ripples that ever widen around it are the effects you will have on the world. The more complete you have become as an individual, the bigger the stone you will be, and the more powerfully your ripples will impact the world pond.

The ripples start in small, tight rings. Imagine them to be your family, those closest to you. Your splash affects them the most. What you do, who you become, and how you conduct your life will determine the quality of their lives too. The better and more complete you are as a person, the more able you will be to offer them the great currencies of life. Love, support, generosity, a positive outlook, enthusiasm, excellence, compassion, understanding, and joy—all of these are life currencies. They mean something. They are valuable and sustain a great life—not only for you, because you possess them, but for those around you. You are able to give what you have freely to others.

The next rings out are your friends and coworkers. They, too, will be strongly impacted by you. The next ring of ripples represents your community and what you are able to bring this group. The next ripples will represent your country. Finally, your splash will ripple out to the world itself.

> *"The only things you live to regret are the risks you didn't take."*
> —*Unknown*

Your view of yourself in relation to the world is probably narrow. You may view yourself as not being capable of having a large impact on the quality of life or direction in which the world will go. After all, you are just one person, and one person cannot change world events. You absolutely can! The world is made up of nothing more than individuals who have planned and directed their lives and goals in such a way as to become big stones that make big splashes. The world starts with just one person. Then we add another and another until we have the globe populated with individuals whose actions and contributions impact each other. Each individual has the same capacity to impact the world as the next. *You absolutely have the power to change and impact the world.* It will be solely be your choice as to how you will do that. Will you choose a negative impact or a positive impact? The quality of the impact depends on how complete and successful you are as an individual.

Now trace this process backward one more time. The quality and completeness that you attain as an individual depend on how well you know yourself. They depend on what path you choose to take in life and how you wish to use the genius and gifts you brought into this world with you. This path requires the excavation of the genius within you. The way in which you excavate your genius requires you to examine your talents and skills and determine how you will support your genius. How you support that genius requires a plan or design. That design requires you to make long-range goals and short-range goals. Every bit of this begs you to make choices for yourself. A choice needs the awareness that the choice is yours to make or ignore.

How far backward can you go here? You can go back as far as today. Right this minute, today, the choices you are making have the potential to affect the whole world. You can choose to share your genius with the world and impact it positively or not. You can choose to live your best, most perfect life or not. You can choose to become an independent, complete person or not. It is all up to you.

Just understand that you have immense power within your control. You are not helpless or at the mercy of the world. You may choose to exercise that power or not. The power lies in choice—*your* choice. It is as simple as that—the power of one choice. Be aware of what you are choosing.

How huge is that? Do you feel overwhelmed by it? You shouldn't. If you do, go back and read the book again. It is simply a matter of designing the best life for yourself that you can design—one that utilizes all of your talents, all of your skills, all of your likes and dislikes, and of your potential. In choosing this path, you will find passion for your life's work. That passion will ripple out to those around you. Because you have passion and excellence in your work, along the way you will become abundant, and you will be able to share all the forms of abundance that a complete person brings to life. You won't have to *try* to affect positive change in your family, friends, community, and the world; you just will. The ripple effect of you living your best, most perfect life possible will do the changing. You simply do the choosing.

The best part of all this is, it is all within your reach. I have shown you how important you can be in the scheme of things. See yourself as important and valuable. See yourself as capable and special. There is, after all, only one you with your particular gift in this whole world.

Dream as largely as you can. Don't allow yourself to indulge in limits. Set goals and work toward them. Invest in yourself by taking advantage of the education you are being offered right now. Keep asking yourself what you can do on an everyday basis to support the goals you make. Practice goal- setting and chunking down those goals so that they are not overwhelming to you. With each goal you achieve will come a confidence that you can tackle anything and achieve anything. You will begin to discover how really capable you are. This whole process of living the perfect life starts with simply making one choice today with awareness.

I hope that you get everything you want out of life. I want you to live your life to its fullest and enjoy every minute of it, even the minutes that aren't so wonderful. It is all part of the experience. I am living my perfect life and am expressing my gift at this moment. I began with a dream of making just one person's life better and more successful. I chose to become a life coach because I was called to it. I have passion for it. I have the gift of seeing the genius in people. As a practicing life coach, I get to live my passion every day. I hope to inspire you to use your genius and to gift us all with your genius.

"When I stand before God at the end of my life I would hope that I could not have a single bit of talent left and I could say, 'I used everything you gave me.'"
—*Erma Louise Bombeck*

About Coaching

Coaching is a unique partnership between client and coach. Hiring a coach is embarking on a journey that moves your life forward from where you stand today to where you wish to be in your tomorrows.

There are literally thousands of life coaches around the world who can help you turn your dreams into goals that are achievable. They do this, not because they know all the answers, but because they know the questions that will unlock your personal brand of genius. Coaches don't pretend to know what's best for you in your life. You're the expert in that area. But they do have the tools to bring you clarity and the structures to help you accomplish anything you can dream. A coach *cannot* and *will not* do your work for you. They *can* help you navigate the roadblocks that might have otherwise stopped you.

Coaching is like having your own personal angel on your shoulder. A coach supports you, encourages you, and helps you devise your own personal life design. It is a unique experience and has moved thousands of people just like you forward into lives that are more fulfilling and authentic.

If you think you could benefit from hiring a life coach, but don't know where to find one, you can search the Internet under "life coaches" or "life design." Find a coach who specializes in the area of your life that you wish to improve. It can be anything from uncluttering your life to relationships and business.

If you think you might like a career in life coaching, there are several great schools of coaching. I can highly recommend my alma mater, the International Coaching Academy, located at www.icoachacademy.com. Or, you can search the Internet for coaching schools.

This book may be purchased in your local bookstore, on amazon.com, or by Internet at www.youcouldbeanything.com. Discounts for bulk orders are available and vary depending on the size of the order.

For more information about coaching or hiring Jeanne Webster as your coach, please go to www.youcouldbeanything.com. Ms. Webster takes only committed clients who are willing to participate in the minimum of a six-week program.

If you are looking for an exciting guest for your next event, here are Ms. Webster's most requested speeches:

Evolving Parenthood
Mentoring and Coaching Teens
You Could Be Anything and You Are More Than You Dream

Ms. Webster also gives workshops and seminars to teen groups and to teens with parent partners at conferences, or for private organizations.

For further information about availability and fees, visit Ms. Webster's website: www.youcouldbeanything.com.